CHINESE DIARY & ALBUM

CECIL BEATON

Chinese Diary & Album

With an Introduction by Jane Carmichael

HONG KONG
OXFORD UNIVERSITY PRESS
OXFORD   NEW YORK
1991

Oxford University Press

Oxford   New York   Toronto
Petaling Jaya   Singapore   Hong Kong   Tokyo
Delhi   Bombay   Calcutta   Madras   Karachi
Nairobi   Dar es Salaam   Cape Town
Melbourne   Auckland

and associated companies in
Berlin   Ibadan

Originally published by B.T. Batsford Ltd. London as Far East,
1945 and Chinese Album, *Winter 1945–46*
This edition arranged and issued, with permission and
with the addition of an Introduction, by Oxford University Press
and John Nicholson Ltd. 1991

Arrangement of text and photographs
© *John Nicholson Ltd. 1991*
Introduction © *Jane Carmichael 1991*

Cecil Beaton photographs Crown copyright reserved 1945,
1946, 1991

Cecil Beaton text © *the Beaton Estate 1945, 1946, 1991*

The collection of some 7000 photographs held by the Imperial
War Museum, London, comprises the bulk of Cecil Beaton's
work as an official photographer during the Second World War.
Visitors are welcome to consult it in the Department of
Photographs and prints may be ordered on application.

First published by Oxford University Press 1991
Published in the United States by
Oxford University Press, Inc., New York

ISBN 0 19 585428 4

British Library Cataloguing in Publication Data
and
Library of Congress Cataloging-in-Publication Data
available

Designed by Pages Design Services
Printed in Hong Kong by Skiva Printing and Binding Co., Ltd.
Published by Oxford University Press, Warwick House, Hong Kong

Contents

Introduction

WHEN the books *Indian Album* and *Chinese Album* were first published, they were introduced as showing:

> ... countries, now awakening to a new importance in the affairs of the world ... seen through the eyes of a great artist with the camera.

For seven months in 1944, Cecil Beaton had been commissioned by the British Ministry of Information to travel as its official photographer in India and China. His photographs, despatched by uncertain routes from the jungles of Burma and the hillsides of China, were used in the contemporary press as part of the official policy of familiarising the British with the more remote theatres of war. On his return, Beaton produced an illustrated account based on his diaries and photographs, entitled *Far East*. But relatively few of the 4500 images he had taken could be included and so in the winter of 1945–46, the two 'albums' were compiled and published. They were at once recognised as containing some of the best of his work.

The Second World War challenged Cecil Beaton as nothing had ever done before. Born in 1904, the son of a well-to-do timber merchant, he had set out deliberately in his early twenties to establish himself as a darling of society, a leading portrait photographer, an original theatrical designer and an amusing writer. It says much for his powers of determination that, by his mid-thirties, he had largely succeeded. However, he was far more at home in the drawing-room than the military barracks, and it was one of the most surprising turns of his career that he should become a noted war photographer. Official photographs were taken under the auspices of the propaganda organisation, the Ministry of Information, and the services themselves, as part of the effort to publicise Britain's cause at home and abroad. A friend of Beaton's, Kenneth Clark, the Director of the National Gallery in London, was involved in the Ministry and suggested that his photographic skill could be useful. Unlike other official photographers, Beaton's work was not submerged in the usual cloak of anonymity; his standing ensured that he received a personal credit and his commissions were specially arranged. In 1940 and 1941 he was busy on the home front showing the engagement of the civilian and the role of the Royal Air Force. In 1942 he undertook his first foreign tour, travelling to North Africa to photograph the war in the Western Desert and to the countries of the Near East to portray their leading personalities.

His photographs and book, *Near East*, met with general approval and prompted the Ministry to plan his most ambitious commission, the journey to India and China to gather material on these little known theatres of war. Between January and July 1944 he covered enormous distances, visiting the Burma front, travelling extensively in northern and central India, and then flying over the 'Hump', the air route over the Himalayas, to Chungking, the wartime capital of Chiang Kai-Shek's nationalist China, and from there touring the southern provinces of Szechwan, Hunan, Kwangsi, Fukien, and Chekiang. He swung between the extremes of luxury in the Viceroy's residence in Delhi and the acute discomfort of travel by dilapidated army truck through China. Assessing the experience in his diary he wrote:

> It has been just what I needed, and the toughness of the trip has been beneficial too. For it does no one harm to get tired and to walk too much, to be either too hot or too cold, to go hungry for a few hours. I am heartened to realize how well my constitution stands up to these tests. But I have become painfully conscious of my limitations and mental weaknesses.

But in writing this Beaton was doing himself an injustice; he overlooked the austerity and discipline which the war placed on his photography, stripping it of much of its previous drawing-room glamour and forcing an altogether less self-indulgent and more candid style. Never very interested in technical wizardry, his preferred camera was a Rolleiflex, a twin lens reflex which took two-inch square negatives and was convenient and robust enough to survive the rigours of travel. It allowed him sufficient flexibility to encompass the casual and the formal. Portraiture dominated his work and, where possible, he liked the sitter to pose to his instructions, but his studies such as those of the coolie boys, the merchants, and the schoolgirls in India, or of the destitute, the children and the workers in China, are simple and direct and far removed from the fantastic style of his pre-war days. He was not and did not pretend to be a war photographer in the conventional sense of setting out to compile a visual narrative of the effort and cost of battle. In this sense he was right to recognise his personal limitations, but he overlooked his strengths; his sense of beauty, both physical and natural, his ability to capture the play of light on form and texture, and his eye for a satisfying and serene composition which gave his photographs an appeal which reaches beyond their wartime context. Beaton was intensely conscious of human dignity and his style emphasised the attractive, not the abhorrent. It was an idiosyncratic record of countries at war, but none the less valid for that.

Surprisingly, Beaton tended to disparage his gifts as a photographer, feeling his skills as a writer whose output numbered more than thirty books, and as a theatrical designer whose work included the brilliant costumes and sets for the musical and film, *My Fair Lady*, were somehow 'worthier' than something which came relatively easily. But photography was the consistent backbone of his life. In the late forties he was seen to have matured and although his society portraits were often studies in perfected glamour, he retained the lessons of his wartime work and had the courage to be simple when it suited. His distinguished contribution to artistic life was recognised with a knighthood in 1972 and he died on 18 January 1980.

Later in life he recognised more clearly the importance of his official photographs and described his reactions after a visit in 1974 to the Imperial War Museum where most of them are preserved:

> Looking at them today, I spotted ideas that are now 'accepted' but which thirty years ago, were before their time. The sheer amount of work I had done confounded me.

As interest in Cecil Beaton and the diversity of his talents grows, this timely re-issue of his wartime 'albums' can be enjoyed for the insight they give into his development as a photographer and as a record of his response to the beauty of the countries he visited at a crucial stage in their development.

Jane Carmichael
Keeper, Photographs
Imperial War Museum

January 1991

Chinese Diary

To
DIANA COOPER
With Love

Preface

MANY people during the last few years have made fantastic journeys to the far corners of the Earth at record speed. My feats were not extraordinary. But it is possible, I think, that some readers may like to escape with me for a few hours from their everyday surroundings and share the superficial impressions of a traveller who visited for the first time, and in wartime conditions, some quarters of the Orient. I can promise that they will read nothing of politics. Gandhi is not mentioned here. Nor will they find any attempt to solve the Indian problem. Too much criticism has been aired by others — little of it constructive.

This is not an official book. The views expressed are my own. I was sent to India and China by the Ministry of Information as a photographer. It was agreed before I left that any writing I chose to do was entirely my own affair.

I wish to thank all those who received me so patiently and, often in trying circumstances, showed me so much friendliness.

C.B.
April, 1945.

Riverside blossom

CHAPTER ONE

To China

O NE of the most prodigious of all war feats has been the establishment of an air-service from India over the Himalayan Mountains to China. This traffic continues in the face of appalling hazards, day and night, in all weathers, through the year. No journey could be more difficult and dangerous. If the pilot should get lost, it is impossible to map-read the course; the route is crowded and collisions have been frequent. Violent electrical storms toss aircraft about mercilessly, causing civilian passengers to utter panic-stricken screams as a draught throws them up two thousand feet, or worse still, drops the plane as if it were a stone, and there is not always that much space to spare. The pilots know that to clear some of these peaks they must fly at an altitude of between twenty and thirty thousand feet, and that the failure of one engine means disaster. "There's a mountain straight in front of me," a pilot was heard to say over the radio, "but I guess it's too late." Often the cargo is such that it cannot be jettisoned to lessen weight in case of emergency. There is no place en route for a safe forced landing. Often the trip is made flying blind almost the whole way. From the number of colleagues they have lost, the pilots know that the odds against them are high, but they keep up these trips over the "Hump", conveying all passengers, cases of medicine and currency, every bullet, grenade, spare-part, rubber tyre, jeep or six-wheel truck — everything, in fact, which is brought into the country. Thus China today is receiving more aid than ever came to her along the Burma Road.*

* April, 1944.

At the airport I sympathised with the Chinese civilians who sat awaiting the "take-off" in the heat of an Indian summer day, for they were wearing three suits apiece. Although the Indian officials are smilingly tolerant about the regulation that only one suit may be taken into China (where clothing fetches prohibitive prices), the Chinese could hardly have started peeling off their layers of Harris tweed.

We climbed very high in the air; the vast mountains, under a covering of icing-sugar, appeared on the port side to be very much higher than we were flying. Most of the passengers were extremely sick and made horrible noises into paper bags. After a bit, the American sergeant sitting next to me said he wished we'd bump more, as it was very exciting. I soon envied the Chinese civilians their extra suiting; one's clothes suddenly felt flimsy; it was getting very cold in the airplane. I tried to sleep — couldn't — tried to read — couldn't. I looked from the windows, grateful for the soothing colours of the cloudscape, but I did not like the rugged mountain peaks still soaring above us. I stopped looking. The sensation in my ears warned me we were flying higher. I felt dizzy and uncomfortable from the height of twenty thousand feet, and I wrote down some of my impressions with a wobbly hand:–

"Eyes watering — head lolling from side to side — no energy, mental or physical — a tingling in hands — chest pains in spasms — snow mountains — snow clouds — sky prismatic rainbow colours — scratch ice from windows — 20 degrees below zero — headache like neuralgia — as day advances light on mountains rosier and shadows more pronounced."

The second pilot came along with oxygen tubes, and said we should share out and take turns. It was a relief to breathe deeply into these masks, and to fill one's lungs with the warm rather onion-scented air. By degrees the light went out of the day. Evening — then night and blackness. The drumming in ears indicated one was flying lower. A few sparse twinkling lights below, in irregular designs, signified that we had almost arrived. It seemed we stopped moving in the air, so slowly did the engines run. We now descended through gorges, avoiding the mountain edges and the electric cables running above the rivers, and, once again, had grounded. Sounds of relief from all, including gutteral noises from the Chinese. The pilot said he thought he had seen Japanese aircraft making towards us before we had escaped into the clouds. I was glad he kept us in ignorance at the time. Not a moment was lost unloading our precious freight. Lorries dashed alongside and within a few minutes were loaded and on their way.

During the following weeks I travelled five thousand miles by truck, sampan, train or airplane. I was given many opportunities of seeing conditions in a country that, apart from the limited air traffic, for years has been cut off from the outside world. Valuable as this air link is, it cannot have an appreciable effect on the four hundred and fifty million people of China. While the enemy is in control of over half her important cities, rivers and railroads, it is as difficult for a foreigner who visits the free territory to get an impression of the real China, as for a traveller to judge America from the Ozark Mountains of the Middle West. All the Europeanised cities, in which, it is agreed, Chinese culture flourished most, are occupied by the Japanese. With the possible exception of the University town of Chengtu, in none of the cities that we have come to hear so much of in recent years is there opportunity to develop the arts of living. Leisure is limited. Few enjoy any comfort. The wealthiest in the land rarely have an opportunity of showing signs of luxury. The West of China consists of the agricultural and more mountainous provinces in which transport has always been poor and existence hard. Life in these paddy fields and small dark villages can have changed little with the passing of the dynasties. From early childhood till oldest age, from dawn until dark, every day of his life, the labourer toils for the minimum reward. The carrier-coolie, his head bent sideways, minces like Agag, under his appalling load. The farmer, almost naked, with legs as muscular as Nijinsky's and wide apart as a wrestler's, plants in the swamps, with zealous speed, the small aigrettes of riceshoots. The water-treaders at the wheels, covered with sweat, defy by the hour the laws of gravity and cause water to run uphill. The river coolies, in the rain, wearing the short capes of palm-tree fibre that, although of a design thousands of years old, are distinctly fashionable in appearance, strain at every limb as they fight the unpredictable currents and the evil spirits beneath the water; stolid young women weed in the mire, or thresh vigorously throughout the heat of the day; children, with a wisp of bamboo, drive the herds of goats and gaggles of geese; the old women pick the leaves off the tea trees, or tie little bags, against the onslaught of birds, over the ripening plums. With infinite patience, everybody fights against discouragement and disintegration, and in the face of all disasters their spirit remains unbroken and unbreakable. When others would despair the Chinese smile with contentment, for they are of the Celestial Kingdom. Each farmer, coolie and soldier feels about his lot as did Shao Yung: "I am happy," he said, "because I am human and not an animal; a male and not a female; a Chinese and not a barbarian; because I live in Loyang, the most wonderful city in all the world." Smiles and laughter are never distant; they are the ever recurrent theme that runs through the overcrowded bamboo villages and newly-bombed towns, along the lines of coolies, human beasts of burden, in the curving mountain passes, down the river banks where millions make their homes in flimsy, overcrowded sampans. Smiles appear at the misfortune of others, at moments of terror or anxiety; they are a means of "saving face", are present at both birth and death (the two "great happinesses"). The Chinese sense of humour, easy recognition of the comic and inveterate optimism combine with the national feeling of resignation to help them bear the misery — sometimes cruelly unnecessary — of present-day conditions.

In fact, the silent, inscrutable Chinese, who moves noiselessly and laconically through the pages of fiction, is an invention that bears no relation to the sturdy, boisterous people I saw working for existence. I found the Chinese demonstrative and highly strung, easily roused to excitement or anger. They are apt to blush more often than the English, while a rapid change of expression adds much to the charm of these uninhibited extroverts. White teeth flash; eyes are tightly screwed up in an access of convulsive mirth. I marvelled at the eloquence with which the Chinese physiognomy expresses different emotions, indicating in turn inquisitiveness, surprise, greed, terror or embarrassment. By the grimace he makes, we know how far a coolie has trudged, how rough the way has been, how heavy his load. As he toils up a precipitous slope, his contorted features resemble those of a martyred saint; yet when he reaches the summit to rest for a moment, the expression of relief is beatific. Every police-boy, perched high on a concrete rostrum at the crossroads, gives an heroic pantomime performance. Running the gamut of facial expression, he directs the traffic with the gestures of a great actor. With what scorn does he observe a driver whose engine has broken down; with what unabashed amusement does he witness some ridiculous mishap to a passerby; with what popping of eyes and wild contortion of muscles does he control the ferocious rush of the approaching traffic!

Unlike the "otherworldly" Chinese of legend, contemplating by the hour a bird on a tree or a flower in a vase, most of the people I met were shrewd and business-like realists. And then, one has only to spend a single night in a rickety native hostel to discover just how "soft-footed" the Chinese are! A traveller who wants to sleep must contest against the noise of furniture being lugged over the resilient floors of the rooms above, a Niagara of family gossip that continues outside his door all night, and the singing of a neighbour "in good spirits". The Chinese is no lover of silence — witness the noise in any restaurant, with cooks and waiters hulloaing, babies caterwauling, parties at neighbouring tables celebrating an anniversary, or playing raucous gambling games, with dogs barking, cymbals being beaten and brass bands braying in the street outside.

The Chinese of fiction is always delicately proportioned with an ivory-coloured skin. In reality, he is often husky, squat, with over-developed muscles and a thick bull-neck, and his skin is of a healthy apricot hue. Although the colouring of his hair is monotonous, his appearance otherwise varies to an astonishing

(Above) Salt well

(Left) Underground war factory

(Below) Making radio transmitters
        and naval dockyard

The paddy field

extent. His mouth, being finely chiselled, is his best feature (just as it is an Englishman's worst), and his eyes, which seldom show any lids, turn down at the outer corners.

Pidgin English is scorned and seldom heard. If the Chinese speaks the English language, it is apt to be with grammatical perfection, a much wider vocabulary than the average Englishman employs, and possibly a strong Chicago accent.

During the last painful years China has struggled on, in spite of appalling shortages of equipment (including heavy weapons), transportation (including fuel) and all sorts of medicines. The Chinese genius for the makeshift has stood her in good stead. As the Japanese approach, the Chinese tear up the railway lines to make them into guns. The scarcity of petrol has promoted the discovery that trucks and lorries can be run on camphor, alcohol, locally produced wines and spirits, and on crude oil made from the Tung nuts that grow on the hillsides. Lorries, that might have been considered to have done good service after travelling these roads for a twelvemonth, are, after four years, in spite of the non-existence of spare parts, seen hurtling along the mountain passes with seven separate pieces of outer tyre bolted on to their wheels; the driver bangs frantically on his door to warn pedestrians, for the horn and brakes are missing. As the truck vanishes round a hairpin bend the the air is filled with a pungent reek of moth-balls — anyone who has travelled in a camphor-run vehicle for a few hours is recognisable for many days to come.

Merchandise is floated down the rivers on improvised bamboo rafts. The winding roads to the forward areas are flanked by a chain of human carriers,

whose strength and tenacity enable them to cover one hundred miles of rough mountain path in four days. Young boys of the Transport Corps in pale, chutney-coloured uniforms, with straw-sandalled feet, stagger along under heavy yokes. Old coolies in huge hats, protection alike against sun and rain, push a small mountain of salt on their wheelbarrows, mules are saddled with baskets, tiny Chinese tots become charcoal porters, cows carry coal. The power and endurance of the Chinese is proverbial: troops live for days on end exposed to extremes of cold and heat, sustained by the minimum of rice. When a soldier falls ill, he is the most long-suffering of patients. I saw men, all but dead of Relapsing Fever one day, who three days later had given up their beds to more deserving cases.

The farmer has learnt the habit of complete frugality. In addition to his bowls of rice, he allows himself only a few dice of chopped pork every month. He makes his own oil for the lamp from rape seed, and for fuel, instead of using charcoal. he burns dried grass. Accustomed to disaster, the average Chinese does not worry about his future prospects. Used to suffering, he takes a fatalistic view of personal tragedies. No bad news can lower his spirits for long. As soon as the floods, which have washed away his toil of years, have subsided, he starts to work afresh. The rebuilding of a bombed town is begun almost as soon as the "Raiders Past" sirens have sounded. This stoic power of resistance constitutes a formidable threat to the Japanese invader. Such is the scale of the country that a regular army of six million Chinese operates behind the enemy lines. The Japanese have learnt, to their chagrin, that the Frenchman spoke wisely when he said that China was not so much a country as a "geographical expression".

Throughout Free China, for thousands of square miles, the villages resemble one another in all the essentials. Houses are dark, smoky, with grey walls and black tiled roofs; the inhabitants, wearing the invariable indigo-dyed cloth that fades through so many varieties of blue to pale grey, move about their business in an inextricable confusion of scraggy chickens, pigs, pei-dogs and babies. Sturdy stocky women, over bowls of rice, use their chopsticks like shovels. The walls of old temples are somewhat unaesthetically decorated with stencilled heads of the Generalissimo. In tea-houses of bamboo-matting, the tea-drinkers smoke pipes three feet long, while they listen to the itinerant professional story-teller; a precocious child, who accentuates his points with blood-curdling grimaces and a nerve-shattering clash of cymbals.

In contrast to the darkness and penetrating odours of the village streets, the natural scenery of the country is of an extraordinary grandeur and richness. Fantastic mountains, like upturned stalactites, half-veiled in mist; gigantic waterfalls; hillsides covered with fronds of bamboo or with wild azaleas; ascending pale green steps of rice fields, as eloquent as a flight of steps at Versailles; white wild roses rambling in bridal bouquets alongside a stream, or climbing over a tree sixty feet high; sweet-smelling camphor groves and jasmine — these are the natural luxuries of the poor, in a country vastly over-populated, little industrialised, essentially peace-loving, and seldom left in peace.

Perched on the feathery slopes that rise from the junction of the two rivers, the Yangtse and the Kialing, Chungking, most beautifully endowed by nature, has been made by man into one of the ugliest cities in the world. Although it has the oldest records in China, it possesses no architectural distinction; and the fertile surrounding hills have been defaced with ugly "Golders Green" villas of sooty cement and gritty lavatory brick. Chungking is now four times the size it was before the war; and buildings appear overnight like mushrooms. In the commercial part of the town, some buildings imitate American skyscrapers in ersatz black marble. The poor material of The New Life Compound and its surrounding buildings reminded me of the drabbest days of Russia after the Revolution. Only down the steep steps to the river's edge, where activity is greatest, day and night, do the buildings seem to be indigenous. If the poorest Chinese wishes an extra room in his house, he builds one in mid-air, projecting from the already flimsy bamboo structure. Somehow this system works; the family are seen enjoying their tea aloft, open to the gaze of the world, while they, in their turn, with infinite curiosity, watch the everyday activities below. Clustered together in a "Heath Robinson" confusion, some of these bamboo dwellings are built for only a few months in the year, until the river starts its rise of anything from fifty to over a hundred feet, and the impromptu villages vanish.

The shops are filled with garish needlework, with shoes of good quality, and with tea-sets in dozens, all ugly and tasteless. In the markets, the vegetables are of a surprising emerald green; and in the cafés the macaroni and sugar foods are golden and appetising. Occupants of rickshaws lie back with extended stomachs; the coolies have an aged youthfulness as they run through the mud on flat feet. There is a good deal of money to be made. Even if values have changed, the coolies are richer than before — they are paid three thousand dollars a month — and they carry wads of notes. To lift a grand piano across the river now costs forty thousand dollars.

In the country, every square inch of the brilliant, cedar-coloured earth is cultivated for food. The steepest slopes grow rice, even if the cultivation-strips are only a few inches wide: the swirling outlines of these terraces suggest a painting by Van Gogh.

CHAPTER TWO

Journey to an Eastern Front

AFTER only a few days in Chungking, I left, in company with General Gordon Grimsdale, G.O.C. British Military Mission in China, and Major Leo Handley-Derry, on a tour of the various British Military Missions in Free China. It was an unrivalled opportunity to see much that I could not have seen otherwise. Although we should not be able to visit the front-line armies, we might be allowed within a few miles of the Forward Areas. There was at that time no possibility of visiting the Communist area at Yenan, or areas in Shansi. Here are some extracts from my diary, written en route:–

Kunming. The town is laid out with streets running in the four cardinal directions. There are ceremonial gates, carved pagodas and gilded arches, and an old city wall, now in the process of being pulled down. To-day the Chinese consider walled cities as part of an ignoble past: horrible modern buildings, of no particular architecture, are put up hurriedly instead; thus everywhere there are bogus Spanish palaces and imitation Corbusier banks and cinemas. No rich merchant would dream of building himself a Chinese house.

The jagged mountains, of a limestone so weathered that the outline looks like the temperature chart of a consumptive invalid, are not only of great geological interest, but prove that those extraordinary landscape backgrounds of Sung paintings were, in fact, true to nature. The people here, until six years ago, had rarely seen a motor car, but have now become accustomed to lorries and jeeps jamming the thoroughfares, and to the sound of airplanes, which day and night fill the air as they bring in supplies from the remote outside world.

In the seventh year of war, most people seem to have given their attention to rebuilding and the interests of their family. Only professional politicians are interested in politics.

The air-raid siren sounded; the sky vibrated with the roar of aircraft; but the enemy machines were flying too high to be seen. The crowds trekked to the caves in the mountains. These warrens extend along the entire range and form an impregnable underground fortress; the whole town can shelter here. Nobody showed any signs of anxiety; in fact, the occasion was treated as a picnic; kitchens were set up outside the caves, and the children played organised games.

We went to call upon General Chennault. His room had a collegiate atmosphere, with flags and trophies. We were given cups of coffee — a great luxury. General Chennault, looking like a footballer somewhat battered after a victorious match, sat at a table behind a sign on which his name, perhaps rather unnecessarily, was printed in large letters. No other individual has done more for China in her fight against Japan. Before the attack on Pearl Harbour, his group of American volunteer pilots, the Flying Tigers, had written a wonderful little page of history. Now he is Chief of the U.S. Army Air Force in China: without his contribution, events in the Eastern theatre might have taken a very different course. His task has never been easy; he is always short of aircraft, supplies and co-operation; yet the personal effect he produces is one of wealth and magnanimity. Come what may, he maintains an unruffled calm and creates confidence in others. Formerly a renowned fighter pilot, the inventor of tactics that revolutionised aerial warfare, he knows every aspect of flying from personal experience. After the last war he organised commercial air-circuses that toured America. For five years he was Chief Instructor of the Chinese Air Force Cadet School. At his desk he now deals simultaneously with Washington and Chungking, as he directs the manifold policies and tendencies of his vast organisation.

With the passage of years, he has become a little deaf; his mouth is tight-bitten and turns down at the corners. His complexion, yellow, as if stained by walnut juice, is pitted with deep crevices, and the skin around the jaw and neck is as wrinkled as the leather of the poor quality windbreaker that he wears, with the Flying Tiger painted crudely on the pocket. His black shaggy hair is beginning to be peppered with grey. Yet there is much about him that refuses to grow up. His shyness and utter simplicity are boyish qualities; his Red Indian eyes have a schoolroom mischief in them; and it is only when members of his staff come in that one has a glimpse of the power that he wields so quietly.

He reads their suggestions. "No — that leaves a loophole — phrase that sentence differently, more emphatically. No, you didn't quite get my thought there." He starts to write. Much of his work is now largely a matter of literary composition. The free and easy side of American army life is here exemplified. Perhaps Americans take all generals as a sort of joke — a joke particularly enjoyed by generals — and doubtless are right in doing so. "Hey General," said his secretary. "Hadn't you better put your blouse on?"

"Where's the General's blouse?" enquired some other member of his staff. The cry was taken up — "Where's the General's blouse? Anyone seen a General's blouse? The General's lost his blouse!" At last someone stretched out an arm.

"Here'y' are, General!" And with a wry smile and a shake of his head, the General changed his tunic.

General Chennault

Kweilin. The Americans have a particular knack of making themselves at home wherever they may be. This is not just a question of money. Here, you would think it difficult for them to find anything they could enjoy, there is almost no kind of amusement to which they are accustomed. Nevertheless they chum up with all and sundry — thereby sometimes losing face —

pick up local slang and yell from their jeeps in reply to the welcoming village children. They drink the local rice wine; they organise rickshaw races; for the nonce they are carriers, not carried. Down the centre of the main street comes a stampede: terrified coolies sit back in the place of honour, until the climax is reached with a general upheaval of rickshaws. Dollar notes are brought out in thousands, to pay for the fun and damage.

The English are less adaptable. They maintain, in the face of all difficulties, a completely English atmosphere in whatever distant part of China they may happen to make their headquarters. At all costs they must have food cooked in the English style. Cooking at home is not always of a high standard: it is lower in China. There are certain groups of Englishmen in China to-day, living contentedly in an acme of unnecessary discomfort. Field Marshal Sir Henry Maitland-Wilson is said to have remarked: "Any fool can make himself uncomfortable."

The farther men are situated from any big town, the higher seems morale. Groups of officers, living together in the mountains, who have not seen electric light or tasted liquor for two years, but for whom time has no longer any reality, and who know that it may be many years before they see their homes again, are as free of rivalry, petty jealousy or personal ambition as sailors on a great ship at sea. An enormous amount of magnanimity, tact and patience is shown under exasperating circumstances. Similarly, isolation and the sharing of difficulties have brought about a harmonious and deeply sympathetic relationship between the English and Americans, whose lot has been cast in this distant theatre of war.

Kweilin. Friday, April 14th. Up very early: a slate sky: the anxiety of shaving, dressing and packing: yet we were in good time for the truck that was to take us to the aircraft. But now the clouds were low, and the humped mountains were hidden. Rain started. Thunder crashed through the hills. The downpour was tropical. We sat waiting in our suburban, almost empty, bungalow. The servant girl moved the dirt from one side of the floor to another. We hung around. We made conversation spasmodically. Hemingway, our host, wandered about with wrinkled forehead and a cigarette tight between his lips. He blinked at the rainy window panes. Would we take off under these conditions? The lorry was very late. More rain. Our baggage, neatly packed, stood ready by the door. We read again and again a few old magazines. I unpacked a book. The rain poured down. Leo and I looked at one another in dejection. All our elaborate arrangements for nothing! Wires and signals had been sent — important you arrive such and such a day — but here we were, in a draughty villa, watching the rain beat down on the muddy yard and desolate front garden.

At last a message arrived — no "taking-off" to-day. We unrolled the bedding. Meanwhile the bungalow became cold and excessively damp, but there was not such a thing as a stove or a fireplace. I spent the morning indoors, as on a winter crossing of the Atlantic, wrapped in an overcoat, with a rug over my tropically clad legs. The others went out. The stillness of the empty house was infinitely preferable to the restlessness of the mess room at the British Military Mission. Hemingway returned alone for lunch. We ate hungrily the rations allotted for three. We visited the Consul. He discussed prices. We called on Mrs. Bacon, widow of a Missionary Doctor, who runs a hospital here.

She is over seventy and has lived in the same temporary shack over thirty-five years. She has thick glasses, the thinnest of legs, a bright manner in which Chinese compliments are parodied (your honourable visit to my unworthy house) and a lack of selfishness that makes me feel a swine. All her time and energy are given to nursing and helping others. She is a first-rate doctor and looks after seventy beds in the hospital. The total amount of good that she must have done during her long life is incalculable. She complains about nothing, yet existence is not easy for her. Her junior doctor and assistant had gone off to Hong Kong to buy drugs for her, and had got caught there by the Japanese. I find myself more and more dependent on outside help: Mrs. Bacon provided an impressive lesson in serenity. An Australian spinster has lived with her for many years; but they still call one another "Mrs. Bacon" and "Miss Willcox". They have no radio. On the table I saw a magazine marked — "This is valuable; it has been flown out by air at great expense; it must be sent on to Kweiyang by April 17th and to Hengchowfu by March 3rd." ... Miss Willcox rushed in. "The Rev. So-and-So has a temperature of 105 degrees"; and out ran Mrs. Bacon.

During the next few days, while we remained in the Kweilin bungalow, and the rain poured down and the mud rose higher, the tone of my diary grows more and more depressing. Here are a few further extracts:

April 15*th.* The usual nonsense of no departure; the rain still falling. The Sugar Loaf hills no more to be seen; the clouds, as the pilots say, are "stuffed". Too dangerous for flying, but the hell of it is that we have to be ready for early departure, "just in case", with the beds packed up each time.

The bungalow reverberates with hollow sounds; the rain pours. The mud in the courtyard encroaches upon all floors. I look again at the magazines, at odds and ends, at the pinned up *Illustrated London News* pages on the wall, even unpinning them to see what is on the backs — (advertisements: Huntley & Palmer, Johnnie Walker).

News comes: we will not be leaving to-day, and "so", suggests Hemingway, "what about a game of Camaroon?" I am too dazed and sleepy to read the dice clearly, and we are all conscious that this game is a last resort. I get some idea of how a prisoner of war must feel. The first trapped minutes are the worst.

A dinner party was given, consisting of six British Officers, with four Chinese friends. There were about twelve different courses. A fish that tasted like meat; a meat that was like fish; delicious emerald vegetables; wonderful soups with floating egg wisps in them; mushrooms; young chickens' legs; unidentifiable dishes with unknown savours. For me, the occasion was marred by the toasts that accompanied each course, with "no heel taps". The ceremonial brew, made of orange juice and rice liquor, called Simhwa (three flowers), tasted of turpentine and was rather intoxicating. Chinese table manners differ from our own — rice is shovelled from the bowl to the mouth with fanatical enthusiasm. The *pièce de résistance* of the meal — a huge fish-head — was eaten by one of our guests in a particularly messy way. By the end of the evening the tablecloth resembled a deserted battlefield. Hot towels were handed around; more toasts; a rowdy celebration with crowds who came to watch us from behind a trellis.

Rickshaw coolies ran through mud and rain in large Ascot hats. With their wide-shouldered capes made of bark, which looks like monkey fur, they suggested society hostesses arrayed in the height of fashion. I enjoyed enormously being borne along, through the squelching mud, by someone who looked from the back exactly like Mrs. James Corrigan.

At first it gave me a shock to see one human being being carried by another. But is riding in a rickshaw any worse than being rowed in a boat? Besides, what a romantic effect a rickshaw is capable of producing! No sedan chair, howdah, phaeton, equipage or limousine is more becoming to a woman. I saw a Chinese girl, with rouged cheeks, lying back as she was whirled along, sufficiently near to be of this earth, yet desirable as only the unattainable can be.

Sunday, April 16*th.* If it were not for the fact that escape is impossible, that our prolonged visit is enforced, no doubt it would be interesting to explore the town. But the incessant rain damps not only all one's shirts and one's bed, but one's spirits as well. Kweilin is mediaeval, with its dirt, and the rats which run about the restaurants unheeded; everyone spits on the floor; mediaeval too is the stench of stagnant water, smoke and cooking.

Once more we awoke to a thick mist; the mountains had disappeared in the rain. With no possibility of departure, we took a chance on not rolling up the bedding, and more or less resigned ourselves to life in this empty bungalow.

The wet feet of the servants bringing the mud from the yard outside trampled on one's nerves. A History of China sent me into a muzzy trance; the servants and clerks doing their chores were our liveliest interruption. A strange Chinese woman in Western clothes came in, and sat around; killed time writing notes, looked through the contents of her handbag and sang to herself. I discovered that she works at a hostel attached to a large cement factory. She looked Gauguinesque, like an enormous fruit, and I asked if I might draw her. She giggled; cut chunks off her nails with a huge pair of scissors and sang hysterically. She would not keep still and continued coyly showing off.

In a dilapidated house, rented for a vast sum from the local profiteer, the China British Army Aid Group has its headquarters. The Mess, in spite of its broken down armchairs, ragged magazines and incessant interruptions, might be an extraordinarily interesting place to visit. Most of the men have had tremendous experiences, but are working at high pressure on work of the utmost secrecy so that none of them willingly discusses his work, knowing that the lives of many are dependent on his discretion. I find that, if I have energy enough to get the conversation going on any definite track, the effort is richly rewarded. Few specialists are bores on their own subject; but it makes me self-conscious to talk in a room full of a gallant but taciturn band of officers. I talk to an elderly grey-haired man who says he was a contemporary of mine, and that at my first preparatory school he and Evelyn Waugh were beaten for twisting my arm.

We dined at a Mongolian eating house by the light of one oil-wick. There was a charcoal brazier in the centre of the table, and on this was placed a large earthenware bowl full of boiling water. The table was then littered with plates of the most appetising-looking raw foods — ivory vegetables, viridian vegetables, strips of chicken breast, shining slices of mutton, and small chopped pieces of onion shoots and garlic. Eggs were brought in by the dozen and cracked on the edge of the bowl into the bubbling water; each of us made a fanciful addition to the already savoury brew. We would add a slither of liver, some cabbage, bean-shoots, spinach, mustard or silken chicken. After a few minutes interval, each took his pick with the chopsticks. Not only did the different materials add to one another's flavour, and the ever-increasing fragrance of the stew heighten one's enjoyment; but, having seen the ingredients raw, one felt that the result must be particularly nutritious. One of the British Officers said: "I'm sure after this meal I'll have a wet dream to-night." We were served by a Northern Chinese boy, looking like a wrestler, who brought in successive dishes with a series of peculiar nods and bows.

Through the rain in rickshaws to the theatre. A vast audience sat in the palely lit wooden auditorium, or swarmed on to the sides of the stage. It was a singularly sweet-smelling audience; Russian audiences smell of baked apples, English of mutton; the Chinese do not emanate body-odour, unlike the Indians, the negroes or the French. It was a remarkably youthful gathering. Everyone looked gay and pleased with life; all were busy fanning themselves, eating, talking, certainly amused by the play, but more amused by life in general.

The play, given in Cantonese, with women playing the female roles generally allotted to young men, was traditional, but jazzed-up with the help of elaborate changes of scenery and the inclusion of a saxophone in the orchestra. Although I understood little of what was happening, I enjoyed watching the stylised movements of the actors and the cold precision of their performance; their hands immaculate, not a drop of sweat on their foreheads; for a time I found the noise of gongs and cymbals, punctuating the actors' *bon-mots*, rather stimulating to the nerves. The elaborate costumes were extraordinarily beautiful in colour and design, details of embroidery could be admired even by those sitting in the farthest seats. Female characters were resplendent in filigrees of gold and silver thread and different coloured sequins. The costumes of the young men, in scarlet and yellow and pale pistachio green, might have been designed by Picasso.

After watching three scenes of unintelligible back-chat and clowning, of stylised fighting (like ballet), all of which the audience adored, we went behind the scenes. The *coulisses* of the theatre have always had a magic for me; these, being Chinese, seemed all the more mysterious. I noticed how simply effects were obtained. A sheet of paper, with the rough design of each setting, was the only guide for the scene shifters when they changed the acts. The orchestra was placed in a wooden pen on the stage, while above it sat other instrumentalists, who capped each remark with some clanging noise. The lighting effects were inspired, though the light used was necessarily very weak. Here was the theatre reduced to its essentials, independent of all the drawbacks of 1944.

In the communal dressing-room the cast was changing, repairing their mask-like *maquillage*, eating dinner or polishing up their parts from the script. Ornate head-dresses hung in perfect safety next to a large piece of dried fish; bowls of make-up paint stood on the same table as the actress's meal of eggs and onion shoots; someone was washing his hair in the basin next to the rice bowls. The actors had to fight their way through a dense throng to reach the stage. The barn-like room was lit by only four dim electric bulbs, yet nowhere else have I seen such delicate make-ups. Each face was a work of art, a miniature painting. The pink of the cheeks gains strength as it rises above the eyes; eyebrows are repainted with arcs like antennae; noses most carefully graduated, with an even fineness, a European could only achieve with a spraying machine. Eyes are painted with the fine point of a paint brush. The effect of the lips being pink, not scarlet, is refreshing. This porcelain finish owes something to the fine quality of the Chinese complexion, but more to consummate artistic skill.

The star had that gift, possessed by all real actors, of increasing his stature when he assumed his costume. As a Manchurian prince, he was tall and majestic. At the end of the performance, when he had doffed his magnificent trappings, he seemed small, rubbery and, except for the unusual twinkle in his eye, quite nondescript.

I was busy doing odd jobs, writing notes, with a nail file scraping the mud off shoes, off my tripod, drying or cooking my shoes on the kitchen stove. We were definitely to leave by air to-morrow morning early; the weather would be satisfactory; a four-thirty call . . .

Tuesday, 18*th*. We fidgeted through the night: it was impossible to sleep well with the prospect of having to wake so early. Before four o'clock, the watchman called us. It was dark outside; but we could hear the rain falling. When the day lightened a little we could see the mountains vaguely. But the departure was horrible — I felt quite sick with trepidation, for the rain spurted more viciously than ever, and oozed through the crevices of the fuselage. As we mounted towards the mountains, there were bad-tempered flashes of lightning. Yet, in spite of clouds, in spite of high mountain-tops boring through the clouds, the American pilot triumphed. For the greater part of the way we flew over the clouds; but the moment where we had to come down through them was an alarming one. However, we escaped a collision, flew between the gorges that flanked the Kan river as far as our destination, and arrived at Kanhsien, where thousands of coolies in blue were making an air-station. From my position in the aircraft I could not see why it was we swooped so low over the grass and then shot up again to circle the fields. On the final attempt the runway was cleared of personnel; but the coolies were soon rushed out again to release the wheels of our aircraft which had so soon become embedded in the soft mud. From this point, there are no flying strips, and the journey was to be continued by truck. A young officer, George Dawson, welcomed us. He had been waiting for a week.

We started off on our trip. We had not gone far when we stopped on the bank of a river. But the ferry was held up by a Chinese lorry in difficulties on the opposite side, an excited crowd around its bonnet. Suddenly the engine caught fire. Shouts: the imperturbable Chinese turned very pink. And several

Disabled sailors making sunshades

Rickshaw coolie

Feather dusters

hours passed before we were able to cross, ferried by eight coolies straining rhythmically against long bamboo sweeps. We achieved the other side of the river, and motored through an immaculate town, with exceedingly broad streets and arcades with calligraphic decorations in white and black. This was Kanhsien, wartime capital of Kiangsi Province. The General proceeded to call upon Chiang Ching Kuo, the son of the Generalissimo, the ruler of this town and of four other states. The great man was away, but the visit turned out to be useful. When we set off on our travels again we waited another hour and a half at a second ferry — a bus had got stuck between a ramp and the hill. The ferry coolies and a mixed crowd were struggling to push the heavy vehicle. No success, they could not make it budge. All the while the people inside the bus sat in their places and refused to help. They would wait days on end while someone else did the job, rather than get down. In desperation we decided to stay the night, but the hotel was full; and the magistrate, when we called upon him, invited us to occupy the guest-house of Chiang Ching Kuo, two of whose representatives appeared and asked us to dinner. I had been in one of my cantankerous moods and was rather sour and silent. It was a relief to get a clean lodging, and my spirits improved after I had washed and shaved. In an effort to throw off associations of Kweilin, I discarded all my khaki clothes and brought out my blue suit from my zip-bag. It was extremely damp.

Wherever we went crowds collected around our truck. My camera transformed me into the Pied Piper. The children, who looked like miniature adults and possessed no quality of childishness, recited the English alphabet. The scrofulous heads were revolting and everyone seemed to suffer from an excess of mucus.

During a visit to some American Fathers in a former French Mission, we listened to the Radio news from Burma which had lately been disturbing. The bulletin, though very crackly, was more hopeful — the Japs driven from the Imphal Plain and from Kohima . . . It was strange to hear a priest saying "What a boy!" and using Broadway slang. One, half-shaven, resembled an over-size pugilist, and came from Pittsburgh; another, dark and bright, came from Boston.

We drank orange-wine and left for our dinner-party, walking for miles through the town. Now the arcades, boarded up during the morning, were a blaze of dazzling electric light bulbs. Nowhere else in China are such illuminations to be seen. Crockery and porcelain, musical instruments, filigree silver, toilet preparations, were displayed in a series of brilliantly lit pictures. There was even a bottle of Scotch whisky for sale. Prices are prohibitive; and even so the shop people prefer not to sell, convinced that prices will rise still higher. Leo asked for some camphor tablets which are made here. Each little cube cost ten shillings. The price had risen two hundred per cent.

Our dinner with the Chinese General (all smiles) and an ex-minister (rather gruff) was staged in one of the best and oldest restaurants in the ancient and dirty part of the town. In a room which presented an appearance of tragic poverty, with rickety stairs, peeling walls, old newspapers pasted to the ceiling to prevent the dust falling through the cracks, a threadbare red cloth on the table and old faded paper flowers, we had a banquet of exquisite subtlety and refinement. There were about a dozen different dishes, all equally wonderful. Every course was an event. It did not signify that conversation was difficult. We ate. We toasted one another in dumb show. Particularly delicious was a fish junket (hot) with two heads and tails of fish to ornament the dish; wonderful green vegetables; lotus seeds hot and sweet; liver cut to look like under-the-sea plants; bean shoots, crisp and resilient; a big fleshy fish, unskinned, seasoned with fragrant herbs; and duck soup. Such a feast must have cost at least thirty thousand dollars.

I did not enjoy the rice-wine, which is supposed to resemble sherry, but which seems to me oily and redolent of nuts squashed in turpentine. Mercifully our hosts did not insist on our drinking ourselves silly; and the evening ended a few minutes after we had finished the sumptuous repast. As we emerged, the night air was full of every sort of whiff, including opium; and a woman was buying one of the long straw tapers to light her way home into the country. Our guest-house (built without a lavatory or bathroom) proved to be clean and comfortable. For the first time, in what seemed an eternity, I went to bed knowing that I should not be cold.

Wednesday, April 19th. Leaving Kanhsien (also spelt Kanchow, then pronounced Ganjo) we were thrown out into the vast outdoors of China. Perched high on the truck, open to the air, sun, and the varying elements, we had a wonderful view of how the peasant lives in the heart of this unspoilt country. It was springtime; and the scenery looked unbelievably fresh, of an infinite variety of greens, from the pale pristine shoots of the ricefields, banked up in a succession of swirling curves, to the dark viridian squares of the rice nurseries. From the air this neighbourhood had reminded me of an abstract painting by Frances Hodgkins — cocoa colour, rose-pink and pea soup green. On the ground it seemed entirely green — lucid and touching greens — except for the blue distances of mountains and blue-clad peasants.

The day produced a variety of impressions: of large mountains covered with acacias, and trees with aromatic perfumes; of forests that smelt of sperm, of the very juice of spring; of peasants ploughing with buffalo the waterlogged fields of rice, the mud stretching up to the calves of their muscular legs, their thighs powdery with dry flaky mud. Occasionally we saw an old man being carried under the canopy of a sedan chair. The villages were of smoked wood and dark matting. The farmhouses, with dragon roofs curving at the eave-ends, were simply built and beautifully proportioned. Bowls of rice were eaten under the shade of a straw-plaited awning; the children had exposed behinds, and their parents, as if emptying a pot, often turned them upside down.

We had a picnic lunch of bully beef outside a small town. While the others dickered about for some oil for the truck, I went to sleep in the sun, a hand-kerchief over my already burnt face. But, of course, there was no oil for the truck; we turned back to a hostel to drink tea. The General suggested we remain the night here, but Leo warned us that all our plans would go wrong if we did not reach Kanchen to-night. So we proceeded. As it turned out, the distance was too far for a comfortable arrival before dark; and no one in their right senses would choose to motor by night in modern China. Bridges are broken, pot-holes become craters, and there is often the risk of bandits.

Rain clouds appeared, soon to deluge us; and we had to cower under the canvas covering of the truck. The light went. We drove on in pitchy darkness. Eventually we arrived at a hostel filled with a roaring mass of Chinese humanity. We were all pretty tired after such a long journey, and I was exasperated by the incessant throat-clearings and spitting of our fellow-guests. While attending our evening meal, a waiter spat with gusto out of the window — another spat heartily in the passage outside my room. All night long I heard babies crying, people spitting and heavy footsteps on bare creaking boards.

Thursday, April 20th. Terrific noises in the early morning. Fresh spitting and renewed guttural throat-rasping. A grey day. We performed the ritual of packing bed rolls, loading truck, then went off to the Mission for a wonderful breakfast of home-cured bacon with Irish Catholic priests.

The Bishop, with amethyst ring, in purple and black, seemed pleased to see us. He described the experience during the months when the Japanese, who had taken this town, were installed in the Mission compound:

"A number of people had come to me for safety," he said. "We were quite a large party for supper. Suddenly a little fellow with knife and gun, eyes blazing, rushed in and snatched the cloth off the table, with all the supper things on it! Heavens above! The clatter and crashing were enough to waken the dead! We all got a shock, for we hadn't been expecting the Japs just yet. We thought they would come in at the main entrance; but no, they came in by the back. Well, we didn't know if it was our turn next." The Bishop laughed, and as he did so, his denture slipped. "Oh, there's a holy uncertainty about my teeth," he remarked in an aside before continuing his story. "The little Jap fellow began to pick up every plate, cup and glass that wasn't broken, and proceeded to make amends. Some of the children started to cry. Just as suddenly as he had come in, the little Jap rushed out. Later, when the Field Commander arrived, it was very difficult to make him understand that I was Irish; but he must have given orders to leave us alone. But all the time the Japs were here we didn't know how they'd behave next. Some midget would point a gun at your chest, and you never knew whether it would go off — if it had, it wouldn't have cost him a thought. But they were so mean! They'd do such mean things! Anything valuable they'd destroy. One man came in with a hatchet and with three strokes wrecked my typewriter. Another came in with a gun, looked around, and shot the clock. They'd search you and take anything they had a fancy for. They lifted my watch, my fountain pen, and then before leaving the room, kicked me in the stummick. They're little men too, and they know it. We got on to some of their ways. They won't humiliate themselves in front of foreigners by standing on chairs or a table; so if you want to hide anything you put it on top of a cupboard." The Bishop shook his head wisely, and then nodded as a grave afterthought. "But I am glad I was able to help by being here — worse things might have happened, I declare!"

"Did they loot the place before leaving?" I asked.

"They took everything they could lay their hands on. The village was bereft of everything — as if the locusts had come. On the last night here they ordered everyone out of the village and then set fire to it. Why, the blaze would have pleased the soul of Nero! He could have gone on fiddling all night. Unfortunately there was a wind and this carried the sparks and burning timbers hurtling through the air; and, although we fought the fires in this compound, the rafters caught in the Chapel — one thing leads to another, and by morning all that remained was the little outhouse."

The roads wound around mountains and ravines. Everywhere the peasants were hard at work. After being amazed at what we took to be the sound of a flock of startled geese, we found it to be the noise of wheelbarrows being pushed along the roads. Coolies seem to like this appalling din: perhaps they think it drives away devils; never would they waste grease on oiling a wheel, with the result that the shrieking of unoiled axles resounds throughout the country. A door, too, is all the better if it possesses a squeaking hinge.

From Kiangsi Province we had now arrived in Fukien Province. We were trying to make our night's stop at a small place named Kien-Yung. Picnic lunch by a river; the Chinese cook had forgotten to boil the eggs, so we ate them raw; an idyllic setting; but soon the rain started. Crouched underneath the tarpaulin in the back of the truck we could see nothing of the soused country-side, but were almost asphyxiated with fumes of carbon monoxide spurted out by the exhaust. The rain poured — then stopped. The hood open, we again surveyed the open Chinese landscape — bamboo, rushes, mountains, rivers, paddyfields. But, once more, the rain began: once more we were condemned to semi-asphyxiation.

Saturday, April 22nd. A night spent in a Chinese Temple came to an early end. Most of us were up by four-thirty. I was in the rearguard at five-thirty. By degrees I am getting accustomed to sleeping on a wooden board; but the pelvis is apt to become painful if one lies on the face too long; I find the skin is peeling on my left hip-bone; a pity I am not fatter. We set off before six o'clock, two trucks following in case we should break down.

Our route to-day took us through the mountainous paths of Chekiang Province. No country could be lovelier. Gigantic gorges and vast mountains in the distance. When seen close at hand, they are covered with every exotic and strange variety of tree; ilexes in new leaf, with pale stylised foliage as in mediaeval tapestry; bamboos growing like pipecleaners; and there were cascades of blossom; azaleas, mauve, shrimp, scarlet and yellow; a mauve tree covered with waxen trumpets; the flowers of the pummelo bursting from ivory nobs, are the apotheosis of all bridal blossoms, and their perfume is positively celestial. All day, the vistas before our eyes were incredibly lovely and varied; winding rivers, bordered with white rambler-rose bushes and flecked with white shell-like sails; neat terraces filled with gold barley or pale green bristles of rice.

The pathways, made through the mountainsides centuries ago, are still used as shortcuts by the coolies, who push their wheelbarrows, or small carts equipped with a bicycle wheel, throughout the hours of daylight. They look like souls in torment as they lumber past on their flat feet, sweating and flushed under the strain; their life is dedicated to this appalling labour; there are only a few halts to rest or laugh. Someone said, "It's easy for them to die, but their troubles start if they become ill." It was a poignant and upsetting experience to watch this interminable procession of labouring humanity. Even midget children carry loads with an obvious sense of responsibility, and hop out of the way of our truck, terrified but agile. Some of the boys, all dressed alike, carrying swinging baskets, remind one of a chorus in the theatre; now and then the groups of coolies in their pagoda hats and blue trousers look extremely gay and charming. But here is a ghoulish figure staggering along at a tortoise pace, his torso and arms covered with discoloured patches and spots; his yoke makes life a torture to him. It is comforting to think he may pity us strangers as mere foreign barbarians, while he is a privileged inhabitant of the Middle Kingdom, the Centre of the World.

General Li Mo An

Leo, unfortunately, pointed out to me the lavatories in one village, and remarked how much the Chinese enjoy sitting in a public place and surveying the passage of life. After this, not only did I catch sight of hundreds of these primitive arrangements of barrels and planks under matting roof; but a horrible stink was seldom long out of my nostrils. As we sped through them, I learnt a lot about life in Chinese villages.

We lunched at a depot of the British Military Mission in Longchuan. Again I was struck by the pathetic plight of these English youths, planted so far from their homes, in a world of new wood, bamboo, mud and flies. Fortunately, their work keeps them extremely busy, but the visual aspect of their existence is extremely bleak . . . . An Australian took me to see the patchwork of fields from the heights of a hill where we found many graves: a baby wrapped in a basket: a cat. One newly-raised mound contained the victim of the latest village scandal — a woman had been "carrying-on" simultaneously with a soldier and a colonel. The colonel had killed his rival with a sword, made in this town, which is famous for its swords, and the woman was paraded, in disgrace, through the streets.

The next stage of our journey, towards Wenchow, should not have taken us more than four hours to cover; but we are in China; our trucks are old; they have been evacuated down the Burma road and are not meant to last more than a year without new engines; they have not been repaired because there are no spare parts. We broke down. George Dawson, covered with grease, was a most responsible and expert mechanic; but the valves were old; the maintenance people had not done their work properly. We had a glimpse of what travel is like in China during the seventh year of war.

I heard the story of some nuns escaping from the Japs. They drove at night until their truck broke down. During the day the Japs patrolled the road and shot up any moving vehicle. So during the day the nuns repaired the truck under a camouflage of trees, and then on for a bit as darkness fell. For twenty-seven days they travelled thus. It was a pity that we were late. Elaborate preparations had been made to welcome the G.O.C. A guard of honour and a band had been out waiting since early afternoon. These military arrangements, made in such detail, so often end in chaos. The remnant of daylight faded while we were still on the roadside being passed by energetic coolies on foot. We had still over an hour's normal journeying ahead. At last the engine revived. We were greeted by varying outposts. Finally, under a bridge, a line of Chinese soldiers and Colonel Larcom of the British Military Mission, who hobbled on a stick, greeted the General.

A less military-looking assemblage than ourselves it would have been difficult to imagine. All sorts of bundles and servants piled anyhow on the van, all wearing different dress; my face had a leprous appearance under a heavy coating of cold cream against sunburn. Our hosts were extremely business-like and kind. We were presented to a dozen Chinese generals, all looking about twenty, and then conducted into a pretty sampan, newly-built of strong-smelling wood; there were Chinese lanterns to light our way as we were paddled down a river. The Chinese C.-in-C. with a small fat rubber face, enormous nostrils and shaved head, and his staff, welcomed us with the usual exchange of compliments. He might have been any age; one cannot tell the age of the Chinese between twenty and forty. In a dining-room decorated with Chinese and English plaques, bearing suitable inscriptions about Sino-British friendship, and photographs of the leaders of the four great powers, stood a huge table covered with oranges and every sort of cake, a row of large variegated flower vases down the centre. The scene had the look of a Christmas festivity in the servants' hall. Speeches interpreted; more speeches; compliments; tea; everyone started to tuck in with enthusiasm. Suddenly, in the next room, an enormous hidden band struck up the most appalling caterwauling. When everyone stood to attention, I realised this din was the local rendering of *God Save the King*. The noise was so surprising that I could not keep a straight face and felt utterly ashamed of myself for shaking with convulsive laughter.

On each side of me sat a Chinese soldier who spoke no more English than I speak Chinese. Another stampede, when the hidden band embarked upon the Chinese National Anthem. The noises were as if fifty cats had gone mad. I tried to think of all the most horrifying things that could happen — such as the invasion of the room by hundreds of Japanese who would proceed to slash us all with swords — but even this did not prevent my shoulders shaking at the incredible noises.

This little town is full of character. The narrow streets are canopied with curving, writhing, tiled eaves. There are dark mahogany shops, and much busyness of coffin-making, lantern-painting and a lot of shaving. There are displays of tinsel head-dresses for the dead, and fried foods; a good deal of dirt; many aged women; greedy girls with hair-lips guzzling bowls of rice; children with appalling scabies on their bald heads; and old men spinning silk with hook-like hands. It is always interesting to watch Chinese hands in movement; often they are too delicate and small for my taste, but they are always eloquent.

As interpreter I was given a small man with double glasses and frog eyes, who, I was told, had failed in a mathematical examination in English. He was now accompanying me on a visit to the local actors.

A ragged, long-haired group stood around on a very flimsy stage. I wanted them to act for me, but no one could understand my suggestions. The interpreter failed again. I became desperate. I got up on to the stage and acted in the wildest and most grandiose manner; Sir Herbert Beerbohm Tree, the Irvings, Forbes Robertsons, Barrymores, Oliviers and Gielguds had nothing on me. I had hoped that my hamming would inspire the Chinese actors to vie with me. But no — the theatrical celebrities stood around, stunned and dumbfounded. They did not even applaud.

Tuesday, April 25th. A demonstration, involving over a thousand picked troops, was staged for the benefit of General Grimsdale. An inspection; physical exercises, with the Chinese troops falling twenty-five feet from the "Heavenly Gate", performing all sorts of tough manoeuvres and firing from all

Chinese commandos

Cavalry cadet

sorts of guns — the experts said they had never seen such guns before. We inspected the Staff School. We climbed mountain sides to watch five imitation Jap trucks ambushed in a gorge. The programme of events was lengthy. Although the average age of the troops was said to be twenty, most of them appeared to be boys. According to the standards of a crack European Regiment, some of the drill did not appear particularly precise, their uniforms were of a poor material, and their sandals of straw; yet these youths put up a magnificent performance, and at the end of the long day, crawling or running up and down mountains, igniting fuses, blowing up targets, firing guns, they seemed as fresh and enthusiastic as if they had just come on parade.

The two-hour interval for lunch was taken up by a great toasting in local wines; bowing from the waist; a nod and a jerk of the cup; a gulp; another bow; and on to the next man; with a lot of Chinese laughter and gaiety. The Chinese C.-in-C. was justifiably pleased at the clockwork precision with which his day was working out. It was fascinating to watch the contrasts in manners; formality, lack of reserve, rasping voices, picking of teeth and noses, voracious eating, simperings and bowings and scrapings; the sibilant tones assumed by this group of bluff Englishmen.

At night there was a dinner at the home of the C.-in-C., whose wife had helped in the preparation of the banquet. About eight different wines were drunk before dinner — Brandy, Maotai (Vodka), Shaoshing (rice wine made nearby), Saké (Japanese wine off a ship sunk off coast here) and Tiger's-Bones. People's faces became very flushed; there were raucous screams of laughter, bowings, more "no-heel taps" — "Bottoms-up"; the interpreters explained, and yelled with mirth. At length we moved to the dining-room. We sat on stools at a high circular table. The General and his wife could hardly be seen above the white cloth. A relay of delicious foods, said to be aphrodisiacs, was put before us, including sharks' fins and syllabub, all served with a hundred frills and decorations.

Wednesday, April 26th. Tropical rain all night. By early morning the compound was flooded. The river had risen six feet and the water leaked through the bamboo matting on to our papers and on to the bed. Woe is me! My stomach troubles were no better, and I came to know the outdoor lavatory almost as well as my own room. It seemed an eternity since I was internally stable: I could hardly remember what life was like when one was not bothered by incessant visitations to an insanitary outhouse. A Scottish doctor visited me and prescribed M. and B. This had to come many miles; but when it arrived it gave me confidence. I made one short expedition to H.Q. next door, to see some equipment that they had captured from the Japs. Some local journalists were present to answer questions, but the whole procedure was abortive:

"General So-and-So will answer that question, if you will wait." Incessant delays. Most of the information I obtained was at variance with what I had already heard. I was told the Front Line troops did receive, and could send, letters to their family; that they got meat regularly. The rain gushed down and I returned to my drenched shack.

Thursday, April 27th. Pouring rain. The mill-wheel now submerged. We could not leave to-morrow. Everyone in poor spirits, but for myself, the extra day would be a relief, as I felt far from well. I got up to go next door to make a drawing of the Chinese General, but by the end of the morning was thoroughly irritated by the nagging of the interpreter — "General Li wants you to put his stars on this way — Madame Li thinks the neck is too full — Madame Li does not want you to put flowers on her dress." — "Why?" — "She says it's too flowery — Will you do another one of Madame Li?"

Bridge during the monsoon

The rain slashed down. I became rather unnerved as the day progressed, for I had apprehensions, though about nothing in particular; and I felt completely trapped. Would I ever return to Western Civilisation? I visualised the possibility of being taken prisoner by the Japs, and wondered how I would survive the mental ordeal. All these ruminations were founded on nothing more sensational than a telephone conversation with Leo, who rang me up to say he would discuss our plans when we met, but that it was unwise to do so now. I knew that the Jap advance was continuing and that in certain sectors, the resistance was slight. However, in such a vast country there can be no precipitous invasion; progress must be slow. My qualms were the result of some form of nervous exhaustion.

The Return Journey. "You've got a weak tummy still; you'd better come with us." I sat in the front of the second truck. I enjoyed, as a change, travelling with a new set of companions; nevertheless I had qualms lest our truck should break down and I should be unable to join the others at the lunch halt. We retraced our tracks of weeks ago. The azaleas were now over; double roses, *Rosa Multiflora*, like ramblers, had superseded the big white rose, the *Rosa Cathiensis*, of the voyage out. We caught up with the first truck at a ferry. Dr. Young, the interpreter, like the shopkeeper out of "La Boutique Fantasque", in a panama hat and white suit, was very gay, helping the coolies to row the truck across the swirling river. At this halt I had meant to get into the other truck; but at the crucial moment I was taking a snapshot. The first truck went ahead; we followed.

About half an hour later we were halted by an anxious looking Colonel Larcom, from the first truck, standing alone in the mountain highway with an arm raised. At one side of him, a high wall of rock; on the other, a fifty foot drop to the river.

"We've had a serious accident," he told us. "The truck's gone over there. The General's broken his leg."

Scattered about on the boulders shelving down to the river, lay various members of our vanguard. Bits of luggage, suitcases, umbrellas, and pieces of clothing were hanging on the branches of bamboos. Some Chinese boys walked about, their faces marbled with dark dried blood; one of them looked like a prune. A Chinese soldier and Leo, quite undamaged, propped up the General whose leg was giving him much pain. Below, down by the water, lying prostrate on a crag, was Dr. Young, his suit and hat gore-blotched. A few paces below him at the water's brink, on its side, lay the dead and battered truck. That those inside the truck had not been drowned, that no one had been killed, was a miracle. We were told that the truck had hit a large stone, and had jerked over the precipice, before the driver was able to right the steering wheel. The truck somersaulted several times as it crashed down the rocks below; with each somersault, people and luggage were thrown clear. But for a very short snapshot exposure, I would have been sitting next to the driver, inside the truck, in the place occupied by Dr. Young.

I felt helpless: it was fortunate that a Viennese doctor, who had a huge trunk of medical equipment, was travelling with us. Bandages were applied; a stretcher made for the General. Bleeding Chinese lay on the roadside, being sick beneath parasols. Poor Dr. Young was unconscious, his huge boots looking as if they did not belong to his body. The General was brave and smiling. We wondered how he could be dragged up the rocky slope? How to place him in a truck? How could he endure the three hours journey back, bumping over the broken road? No, he must go by river. Someone walked miles to the nearest village to try to telephone for a boat, but returned, having found no telephone. Then someone discovered a boat to go back as far as the ferry. The wounded were piled in. At the ferry, the boatman refused to go farther. Some of our party went off to try to find other boats and boatmen. Mr. Lee, the Chinese radio expert with us, managed to recruit six boatmen; but, although there happened to be fifteen sampans in the neighbourhood, no one would take the risk of allowing his boat to go on such a long journey. I was told that this refusal to help was typical of what might happen in a serious crisis.

We felt very forlorn when, three hours later, the wounded were still awaiting removal from the ferry. At last everything was ready. A boat was launched. The Colonel, badly bruised, could not sit up; Dr. Young was still unconscious; the General was in great pain and becoming weak and fretful. The Viennese doctor gave morphine tablets which did not help enough. A few minutes later the boat returned with a heavy leak. At last it was righted and sent off again.

The river was very high after the rains, and was flowing fast. But it was a slow journey. When, hours later, we passed in our truck the mournful shipload, and shouted from the mountain side, the replies were despairing. They doubted if they would be able to make the hospital to-night; there were rapids; the boatmen, afraid of the approaching dark, had begun to give trouble.

On arrival at the ferry, from which we had started this morning, I felt so weak I could hardly tell the story of our misfortunes. Meanwhile, night covered the unhappy boatload as it moved forward slowly among unknown dangers. We received continuous messages of its progress; it had passed such and such a village; only twenty more kilometres to go. Later, we heard shouts announcing its arrival as it passed a bend in the river, and at midnight it finally reached its destination. The recent floods had been helpful; if the river had been either higher or lower, the journey could not have been made in one day.

The local Chinese General ordered the electric light to be kept on until three-thirty a.m. when the doctors finished work. Most of the casualties were not as serious as we had feared. General Grimsdale would have to be flown back to India to have his leg X-rayed; but he could not yet be moved. A few days later, some of us again embarked on the return journey, leaving behind us many of our original companions. Here are a few more jottings from my diary:

The usual maddening delay at the hostel when we arrived at our destination.

We were tired and dirty, yet it was over an hour before we were shown a room. "You can't just go up to someone and ask for a thing in China," I was told. "You have to wait around, till by degrees, if you are lucky, you get part of your request granted." I was really much too exhausted to enjoy this subtlety.

Father Tiffany, the American priest, lives here, in poverty that amounts to destitution. With the present rate of exchange he can afford to buy practically nothing, no pots or pans. He told us that he is not busy nowadays, for so many of his former activities have become too expensive. He cannot travel: to get a boy to carry his bag on the shortest trip costs one thousand dollars. He lives in a small dark room, without enough light to read at night. He is the one white man in the town.

After living alone for years on end, Father Tiffany is in a highly nervous state and smokes continuously cigarettes which he unsuccessfully tries to roll for himself with dirty fingers. He divined my thoughts: "You feel sorry for me, I know. You see me living by myself with no modern conveniences, having to make continuous effort, muscular and mental. But to you, who come from one of the great modern cities, do modern comforts, hot and cold laid on, constant electric light, give real contentment? You are never alone. Every distraction of the city is available to you. Living among crowds you have no opportunity for thinking; moral values are almost completely ignored by modern society; without religious principles, you are free; you can make love with whom you wish, provided you are not too blatant. When the distractions of one city pall, you fly to another, or to any country on earth. Of course I have spells of great restlessness: I'm three years overdue for furlough now. I was due to leave the day Pearl Harbour was raided. I've been out here eleven years now: but you don't feel remote or lonely after a bit. We didn't get any visitors before the war, except Peter Fleming, and no mail here after the war for two years; they wouldn't accept it at the post office. The first months are the worst, and the year before you know you're going on leave. But what is time? Duration expressed in figures on the clock-face. To my mind, the importance of time varies from childhood to old age; and it matters considerably whether we are considering the present or the past, or looking forward to the future.

There were about eighteen people in our truck, when, at last, we set off this morning. Added to our usual number was a Chinese woman with her family of four small children, their nurse, a picture of gloom and despondency, their male companion, also four students who had not money enough to get to their university. The journey was uncomfortably crowded, dusty and hot; the sun gave us headaches. It was a relief when we dumped the large family at their destination, for the children had become dictatorial. The small boy aged seven had been furious when the miserable nurse drank out of the same water-bottle as himself. "Don't you know rules and regulations?" he screamed.

███████ Every small town and village we stay in is redolent of disease. I am bitten by fleas which, I can only trust, are not plague carrying. Each night I go to bed dreading the horrible strangers that appear in the night. I think and dream of long baths in Calcutta. This morning the Viennese doctor diagnosed the symptoms of one of the orderlies as those of bubonic plague. Macabre jokes. "The Plague Season is on! Have we got a Union Jack? Could we fire a volley with a machine gun?"

My luggage has now become a pitiable mess. My bag, made for airtravel, does not protect any of its contents. The vibration of the truck has caused all the tubes of cream (tooth, shaving and cold) to twist their caps and become perforated; paints have oozed on to cotton wool, on to socks, ties and medicine bottles; my one pair of pyjamas is soused in petrol, and no article of clothing remains undamaged.

███████ I went to call upon two old spinsters, both over seventy — Miss Armstrong, from the West Coast of Ireland, and Miss Wade — in their Mission Compound. They have both been here since 1911, and have lived a fuller life, perhaps, than that they would have enjoyed at home. Here they have become indispensable to the community, treat the local children for all sorts of minor ailments and hold a small court among European passers-by.

While Miss Armstrong sat back, in pain with sciatica, Miss Wade held forth. The non-Christians, the heathens, call her "the Bible Woman", and when she makes an expedition into the country, visiting her pastors, crowds follow her wherever she goes. "They come to see the foreigner, more than to hear the Gospel," she confessed with honesty. "I can walk thirteen miles a day. I generally sleep on a Chinese door taken off its hinges — there are no unwelcome visitors in these boards. You know," she continued, "the Chinese love to pray, they can kneel for hours on end without getting tired — they love it! They come in here from miles around for the four holidays of the year. Christmas is a great time for them."

She sang bits of a hymn, explaining that the harmonium in their sitting-room was so much less strident than the one in the church, but few of the Chinese realised the difference, and they kept this one for their own pleasure.

███████ The truck was crammed. Someone asked, "Could we take three girl students to their school ten lee away?" "Yes." So ten girls turned up. Five were allowed on. Their destination, it transpired, was twenty lee away. We were really very weary. We have travelled over seven hundred miles in this truck. To-morrow, God willing, is our last day of truck travel, and we arrive at Laiyang, the raihead. We ate frogs' legs and filleted eel, but I was too tired and on edge to enjoy the dinner. The bill came to nine hundred dollars.

Monday, May 8th. I was called at four-fifteen for the longest lap of our journey, to the railhead at Laiyang. We have been through a variety of ordeals. We have taken it in turns to sit, in comparative comfort, in the front of the truck; and, when in the back, we have sat on bed-rolls, or stood up holding on to the cross bars while admiring the scenes that fly past so quickly. Ours has been an oddly assorted group. Leslie Shellam, responsible for our comfort and safety, organising our itinerary, paying the bills and taking everything very seriously; Leo, always reserved and stoic; the smiling, happy Chinese driver, never tired, gleefully shouting "Ohay" each time we set off after a halt or setback; Mr. Lee, the young wireless operator going to Laiyang on promotion; another driver being sent back in disgrace for having failed to report that he had venereal disease; and the four students, each with a toothbrush in his breast-pocket, who have spent most of the trip lying asleep on the luggage; somehow they have always managed to get more covered with dust than the others, or maybe it is just because, being originally dressed in black, they show the dust more; their hair has become dun-coloured. In addition to this company, there have been the hitch-hikers from each stopping point; we have taken on five or six at every run. It has been a rough and uncomfortable trip. For this experience, at the present rate of exchange, King George has had to pay out one thousand pounds in petrol alone. It costs one pound to travel each kilometre, and this does not include the oil and running expenses of the truck, or the salaries to be paid to those accompanying us. We have had only the simplest meals, have spent the night in squalid hostels; yet our expenses have worked out at ten pounds a head a day.

A storm broke unexpectedly. The tarpaulin leaked. Everything in the truck became soaked; but eventually we got through to fine weather. I enjoyed standing up as the avenue of trees sped by, and the scenery changed in character. Everything became flatter — patches of dried terracotta earth; fir trees; a few palms; then the plumy tame scenery that I prefer, with smoky green trees perforated by sunlight. A great number of magpies and other birds, shrieks, jays, kingfishers and some huge black butterflies with fat bodies like bats. Everywhere labourers at work. We passed a coal-patch where wretched blackened infants were waddling along, laden with their yoke of heavily filled baskets. We passed miserable looking files of recruits being taken to the war, their guards carrying enormous cutlasses like some weapon out of a mediaeval shadow-play. Some miles farther a fugitive was being chased by a guard with a gun. Both looked exhausted, but all my sympathies were with the fugitive and I prayed that he might escape. At the top of one hill, we picked up an American, working for the American equivalent of our Ministry of Economic Warfare. The charcoal burner in which he was travelling had, at five o'clock that morning, left the village on the border of this province in which we had had our tasteless lunch. We felt sorry for him and gave him a lift.

The roads became smooth and our truck behaved well. We arrived in good time at Laiyang, where the British Military Mission H.Q. consisted of a small Chinese farmhouse, that was in the process of being reconstructed. About a dozen workers were still sawing wood, planing more lathes prior to fixing up walls. A temporary roof consisted of some bamboo matting. Chinese umbrellas, strategically placed, warded off a few of the rain spouts; the ground was a mess of wet shavings and mud. There were a few upright bamboo chairs, half a dozen Chinese clerks were at work in this confusion and some orderlies were carrying on among the carpenters in the half light. By the office-sitting-dining-room there was an open space on to the village lane; and children in various stages of nudity came to stare. The view of the river was blocked by a latrine, built eight feet away from the dining-table.

A former missionary, now become a major, was in charge here. Once again, I was appalled at the discomfort in which these men live. With the exchange so much against us, and the cost of essentials so exorbitant, it seems foolish to economise on extras, and make Englishmen stranded out here work under unnecessarily hard conditions. To a stranger like myself, this house seemed quite unsuitable for a Headquarters. It had been chosen because it was equi-distant from, and comparatively close to, river, road and railway. But it will be cold, damp and dark in winter — in summer, a foetid fly and mosquito trap. The proximity of the village will certainly breed disease.

The Chinese wireless operator, who had been promoted here, was in despair — "I think it's a revolting place," he said. Meanwhile the rain poured down. For discomfort, nothing could compare with this. Only if the temperature had been many degrees colder could conditions have been worse. As it was, there were mosquitoes as well as cold; no glass in any windows, the rain and wind rushing in, the ground so wet that the wood shavings were mashed to a pulp; workmen covering the typewriters with sawdust and clerks idling, as the three young officers conferred under the gaze of the village.

I tried to read: no luck. The noise was terrific. Every upright chair I sat upon was in someone else's way. In the midst of the carpenters' chaos, the cook was preparing dinner and the smoke was such that one could hardly see across the room. The rain poured through the attic windows, dripped through the bamboo matting ceiling with a ping on to the Chinese umbrellas, then with a plop on to the sodden floor. The mud, from outside, was brought upstairs, and on the landing, where about a dozen and a half bamboo beds were strewn with the workmen's clothes. Along the rickety corridor, behind three holes in the wall, our beds were placed. The floor was so unsteady that it sprang up and down at every step.

Chinese general

We were to be called at two o'clock in the morning; and immediately after the evening meal I went to bed. Snores from the labourers: one heard the neighbours talking and their babies crying, as if they were in the room with us. I was too cold to take off my clothes, but so tired that, in spite of interruptions, I was soon asleep. Not for long. The ex-missionary flashed an oil-lamp into my face and, bending low over me, peered through his gig-lamps to see if I were his Chinese orderly. Perhaps it was anger that prevented my going to sleep again for so many hours: that, in addition to the noise of the mechanics talking among themselves. The Chinese are able to sleep through any disturbances. I suppose I must have dozed off eventually; for, when we were called in the middle of the night, it was another shock.

Wednesday, May 10th. The rain bucketed down in angry torrents. By the light of a small lamp we packed our bed-rolls. The trek through the mud and puddles to the truck, half a mile away, did not raise one's spirits. The Chinese do not go out in rainy weather if they can help it, therefore they do nothing about bettering conditions for bad weather. But my depression at having to turn out into this tempest was relieved by the fact that, God willing, we were leaving this dump for ever and ever, amen. On arriving at the station we were told of an hour's delay. But eventually the train was signalled and we trekked through the mud and pools to the far platform. Here there was no shelter. When, at last, we got into the train we were soaked. Our belongings were reduced to a poultice. We all felt cold. We slept sitting bolt upright, but at Henyang we moved to "first class" compartments and lay down to sleep.

My first experience of a Chinese train was not too bad. Nevertheless insistent rain made life seem very squalid. Wherever I looked there were unattractive sights; women disembowelling animals or pulling the skin off eels, squatting to relieve themselves on the rice fields while they picked their noses or searched in their children's hair for vermin. After seven hours we arrived at the rail-end where we ploughed through the mud to the ferry-boat on the river Chang, for a three-hour trip to Changsha. It was here that three great battles were fought in which the Chinese adopted "magnetic warfare" — instead of offering frontal resistance they withdrew and shifted to the flanks and rear of the enemy. The river was so wide that its banks seemed very distant on this dull, grey day. Leslie, our leader, was cheerful in spite of everything, for he holds Changsha tender in his memories. It contains the Red Cross hostel where a few months ago he had met, and married, his wife. He had been walking for eight and a half days when he arrived back to spend the night here; he had been given a hot bath, tea out of a nice cup, bread and butter. His spirits had soared, for there was a lavatory with a plug that pulled. Someone had said: "Let's go over and see the Red Cross people."

"No, I'm sick of seeing Chinese officials."

"Chinese officials! My eye! They're beautiful English nurses."

Leslie had fallen for romance there and then. His wife is now nursing in India, but the place for him is still full of the old magic.

The compound proved to be American. Some Bible Society had built the place ten years ago, at the cost of many millions of American dollars — a number of red brick buildings of no particular character, but comfortable and, in comparison with anything we had known for the last month, with all the latest amenities. Leslie's face was transformed, his eyes like stars, his teeth shining. He received a rapturous reception from the sisters and everyone else working here, including the Chinese gardener. The chief matron called him by his Christian name every second — it recurred like a hiccup.

We were taken care of, fed, given tea, shown our rooms in a doctor's house, and by degrees I returned to normal spirits. To have a bath, wash one's hair, shave, put on a civilian suit, were great events. We had a good dinner in the suburban villa with the nurses. They all asked news in turn of Leslie's "Pat"; till "Pat" became the central character of the evening. Leslie read out some of the dullest passages of her letters, and grinned good-humouredly when adding with a wink "there's a lot more of course". "Pat" had stayed at the Lady Mary Herbert hostel in Calcutta — the Lady Lytton was full. "Pat" had not been able to buy him an English pipe or any tobacco, but had heard there was some at the R.A.F. officers' shop. "Pat" was taking Audrey out for a Chinese meal to-morrow — she would write again. The nurses sat around giggling, or yelling with girlish laughter. Awful jokes were made — "Now, Leslie, what do you mean?" — "Not what you think!" — "How do you know what I am thinking?" — Cups of tea were enjoyed. Most of the nurses wore glasses. One, in particular, was completely unselfconscious and childlike, her face expressive only of amusement and happiness: it is seldom one sees grown-ups so direct, unspoilt and utterly disarming.

After dinner a small Scots nurse came in with a lantern. "I'm having an awful time with one of the Relapsing Fever cases; he's been out of bed three times, and has become violent. I can't find Dr. Wong. Would you look at his papers, doctor?" Dr. Flowers, grey-haired, grey-faced, prescribed some palliative, and the night-sister went back to her work. Suddenly one realised the *raison d'être* of these women here: the background of serious work behind a façade of scones and social cups of tea.

In this hospital, there are over one hundred and eighty beds, where many Chinese soldiers die of fever through lack of medicines. The doctors improvise, try to buy substitutes, but meet with much opposition from the Chinese in control, and often earn more jealousy than gratitude. The big hospital is filled to capacity. Many cases cannot be admitted. The out patients gather in their hundreds and are looked after by the housekeeper. It is only when seeing these Englishwomen at their job that one understands their importance. The social trivialities occupy only a very small part of their existence. For the rest of the day they are Empresses, rulers, with the responsibility of sickness or health, life or death, over large kingdoms. I was very much impressed to hear them all speaking fluent Chinese, and treating their patients, not as strange objects to be stared at (which in a way, I confess, was still my attitude) but as fellow sufferers and fellow human beings. Some of the cases were terrible to look upon; but the nurses did not flinch. There had been no battles lately, and, though some of the wards were filled with soldiers suffering from gunshot wounds, these were mostly cases of carelessness (they hammer on a grenade to see if it will go off, and it does!). But many wards contained the Relapsing Fever cases. This disease had been brought to the city by the soldiers; and now many civilians were suffering from this epidemic caused by lice. The soldiers have no change of clothes; they put on their padded garments at the beginning of winter, and do not take them off until summer. Lice breed in the padding; germs get into the blood stream, affecting the kidneys, and the ensuing torture is excruciating. A high fever produces great weakness. The reason for the shortage of sulphur drugs for curing this disease is said to be that the supplies are being kept against the day when their worth will be even greater than now. The local medical authorities tried to arrange that each soldier coming through Changsha should be given a bath and his clothes steamed, but not enough funds could be found for fuel to heat the water.

The nurses joked about being given notice to quit. "They told us it wasn't safe for women and children to remain here. Put that in your letter to Pat, Leslie! They are expecting the Japs. But we were fooled once before. We sent a lot of our drugs away, and it took nine months to get them back! The Chinese are a great people for rumours; they know everything, true and false. No, you needn't start packing up until you hear the pig-squeal of the carts all night long. Then you know the village people are following the wives of the military officers, and moving off with everything they possess on their carts."

A final cup of tea, and then the great luxury of a big, brass, double bed. I slept so soundly that I did not know anything of the air raid — but bombs were dropped and casualties brought in to be looked after by the night-nurses.

Thursday, May 11*th.*
"Are you sugar or not, Leslie? I never can remember!"
"Yes, it's me that is, but Pat isn't."
"I knew Pat wasn't."
"Well, I wasn't either for two days, but I couldn't keep it up."
A great breakfast party, four more arrivals, three Red Cross officers and a nurse, a lot of stores and luggage, and bomb stories of the night to be told.
"Guess what we had in Hengyang?"
"What?"
"Strawberry tart."
"I could throttle you for making us so envious."
"Pardon."

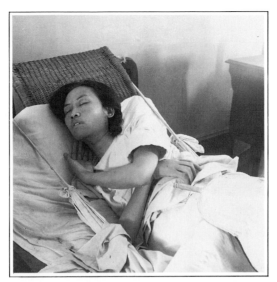

In the women's ward

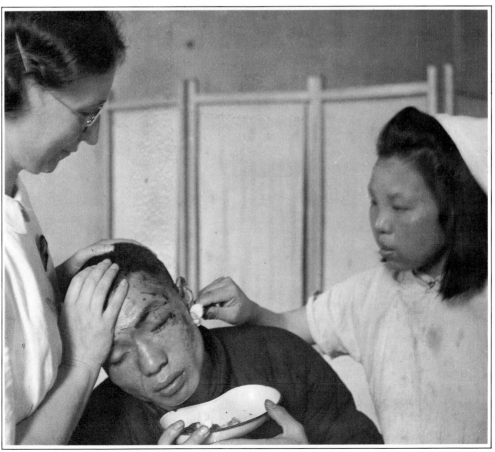

Air raid casualty

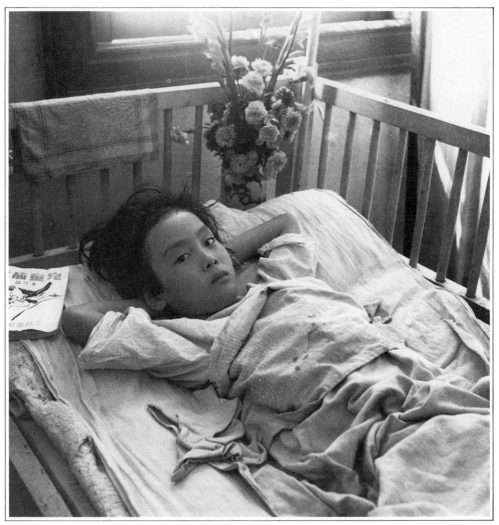

Mission Hospital patient

"You've got the wrong serviette, haven't you? You've the flesh pink and not the rose pink. Now come along with me to the Beggars' Home."

Here four hundred destitutes are being cared for by the municipality. There are no beggars in the town, and most of these people have been brought here, victims of war; they are refugees from occupied China. It is a mournful discovery that these people possess nothing in life except perhaps an old eiderdown, under which at night they lie on a wooden platform — till recently they were on the floor. The old women were far the most abjectly pathetic — bald — some deaf and dumb. Some were spinning at wheels, others looked after revolting babies. The children's class was impressive, lessons were repeated in high sing-song voices, a child of six acting as leader. Some of the nurses and doctors of the Red Cross help to look after these people; admiringly I watched the housekeeper stroking the heads of filthy children, and soothing the forehead of an old woman with fever.

Leo and Leslie took me into the town, but as an air raid alert was on, most of the shops were boarded up. With the official rate of exchange, the prices are fifteen times more for us than for the Chinese; thus some gaudily embroidered satins were one hundred pounds each length, and candles were a pound each. Our craving for sweets led us to pay thirty shillings for a pound of rather ordinary caramels that would cost in England one and sixpence.

Back at the hospital we found Dr. Flowers preparing to amputate a boy's hand. Later I asked him how the operation had gone.

"Oh, after working on the hand for an hour we brought back feeling into the fingers. It was a near thing, but I think the hand can be saved. But the trouble was due entirely to the Chinese belief in the tourniquet. No tight bandage should ever be kept on for more than two minutes. This boy had cut his wrist: a tourniquet of hair had been applied: this had eaten into the flesh down to the bone and had gone septic. So higher up they had tied a tourniquet of string. Higher still the flesh went putrid. Finally they tied a tourniquet up by the armpit!"

Friday, May 12*th.* Even to stay one day in the same place now gives one a feeling of settling down. But after this pleasant respite we must again be on our way: bed-rolls packed at five in the morning. It was with a certain misgiving that we tore ourselves away.

Two American missionaries came out of the darkness to put us at our ease. "Yes, we were expecting you." Mr. and Mrs. H — showed us our room. "Dinner when you're ready."

"Surely it's very late for dinner?"

"Oh, but it's just a question of setting the table again."

Three middle-aged American women, their male counterparts, and a dozen American Air Force ground-staff, were sitting around, rather silent and morose. We ate a good cafeteria meal and joined the community for parlour games. I was amused by the casual way and sing-song voice in which grey-haired Mrs. H — described the disasters that had befallen her:

"Then they told us to quit Shanghai," she said, "and we were six months on the road, held up three weeks some place because of our passports — oh they did terrible things to us! They didn't make it a *bit* easier for us, and we were dive-bombed, but my husband and I were lying flat at the time, and we didn't catch the blast; you know, it's the blast that's bad, you know how it is when a bomb drops. Then my daughter got permission to return to New York, but it took her such a long time to get home — in mid-ocean her ship caught fire and all the crew were too busy attending to look after the passengers, so they tried to get one of the boats overboard, but it went down lopsided with a lot of people in it, so someone cut one of the ropes and the boat fell plump into the water and broke, and everyone toppled over into the water and were swimming around, and some of them got drowned — but my daughter, oh she was all right, she got picked up and taken to Honolulu and they put her on the Clipper to go home — but they had trouble and had to jump for it, but they all had parachutes — you know how it is with parachutes — you just pull the cord. Meanwhile our home here was bombed — all those rooms there in front went, no wall left you see — you know how it is when a five hundred pound bomb drops."

We heard the story of how a missionary woman in a remote part of China had one particular wish — that her daughter, about to be married, should go to the altar in a white silk dress. Where on earth in China, to-day, could she get white silk? God answered her prayers. He sent her from the skies the required article, in the form of the parachute which was given to her, in return for her hospitality, by an American pilot who had baled out after a raid on Tokyo. The only snag was that although she washed and rubbed the silk with lemons, pummalos, oranges and her last piece of soap, nothing could prevent the more observant of the congregation from noticing that, as the bride walked up the aisle, her skirt was marked U.S. ARMY, U.S. ARMY, U.S. ARMY.

Saturday, May 13*th*. After an American breakfast, with plenty of molasses, we left the Mission Compound to learn our immediate fate at the A.A.F. Hostel. The journey down river by sampan was soothing and agreeable after the smells, dirt and bustle of Chinese streets. On our boat was a Chinese soldier being taken to hospital. I have never seen anyone nearer death.

His skin had become greener and more yellowy than his greeny-yellow uniform. He kept groaning, and was so weak that he had to be carried to the top of a flight of stairs where, mercifully, he was put into a rickshaw.

The Americans were in high spirits, said they'd give us a lift to Kweilin, if there was room, next time a transport plane came in. I enjoyed very much listening to their backchat. There are no flies on them. Somehow they manage to achieve a satiny gloss in the roughest surroundings; and even in a remote place like this they organise their comfort on an entirely different scale from ours. Their newly-erected bashas and mess-rooms have a country club atmosphere. Their pin-up girls were cut out of good magazines and really did look covetable. There was a good deal of chatter about mosquito repellent; someone had malaria; everyone must use the repellent to-day. "Not to-morrow, to-day. See that it gets given out — and don't give it to the Chinese; they'll only take it down into the town and sell it."

We enjoyed our stay at the Presbyterian Mission, in an atmosphere of a seaside boarding-house inhabited by Americans. Our hosts were in fine spirits. One of the women had helped deliver twins during the night. Mrs. H —— was busy packing off Bibles by post. Mr. H ——, whose function is to address the packages in Chinese characters, sat back, with large paunch, surveying the room-full through pince-nez, while he fanned himself with a large black paper fan. An old wizened Uncle Sam, who said the grace before meals, and a white-skinned doctor, with an unexpectedly deep voice like a chisel, all joined in the singing of hymns and old folk songs, accompanied by a grey-haired lady in pince-nez and a foulard dress, who hit plenty of wrong notes on the upright. Meanwhile, we had bad luck with the chances of hitch-hiking on a transport plane; and after a time, unable to sustain enjoyment of parlour games and folk songs, we decided to board the next train.

Monday, May 15*th.* Early start for our train. A long and frenzied walk to the station — arrived in great heat and sweat — a slow train leaving at seven a.m. "It should arrive at seven p.m. at Kweilin," some said: others said, "nine". Distance, four hundred miles. Train travelled at snail's pace. To begin with one did not notice stops at every station and meaningless halts in between; then hot, thunderous weather turned to storm; rain poured down and came through ceiling of coach on to the leather arm of my seat — and bugs came out. We killed some with the end of a spoon. Chinese in carriage (second class — no firsts!) spat gutturally, grunted, farted, yawned with the noise of bellowing cows, picked spots on their faces for hours on end or excavated their nostrils, blew their noses in their fingers, then rubbed their fingers on chair-seats or wall. No one had any inhibitions or false modesty; men lying with feet out of windows, women feeding babies at breast, everyone making their own personal addition to the general pandemonium. By degrees the energy, stored up during the night, seeped out of every pore of the body, and I became too tired to read. Leo talked about China. Before the war his firm planted twenty thousand trees: a small proportion were eventually to be used as pit props. They were policed for protection; but of late, this had become impossible. Within a year all the trees had been cut down, stolen, sold or used for fuel. The people are so poor, know so well the horror of poverty, that whenever they can see a rare opportunity of rising above a degree over starvation level they feel they would be foolish to miss it.

The last part of the journey was almost intolerable. We were exhausted. For sixteen hours we had been sitting in the same bug-infested seats. Large bumps arose on wrists and arms. There was not sufficient light to read. At Kweilin North Station we started shunting backwards and forwards. After one hour and a quarter, we were back in the same station from which we had been painfully jolted. The Chinese bellowed, then yawned, emitting every sort of revolting noise and smell. When, more dead than alive, we eventually arrived at Kweilin South, we had to wade through mud ankle high to get to a truck. We came back to Hemingway's villa. I must admit that, by comparison with our various lodgings during the interval, I found it comfortable and even luxurious. To a much larger extent than I realised I had been broken in to squalor.

Tuesday, May 16th. Mr. Priestley is said to have given a talk on the radio about a typical Chinese who spends all his money on some single object of beauty; how, when he walks along the street, he pauses to admire a tree, and a little farther, stops to listen to the note of a bird; how he will spend hours contemplating one perfect bloom. What utter bosh! He is much more likely to espy a particularly large cake of cow-dung and rush to take it home before anyone else gets it!

The evening was a pleasant change: drinks with a sybaritic giant called Fletcher: talk of Vuillard, Bonnard and other such names never mentioned during the last months. It was the first time for weeks that we sat on upholstered seats; gin tasted delicious.

This expedition into the Chinese blue has been an overwhelming experience. It has thrown me back on to my own resources without any aids to escapism. There have been days when I have had nothing to occupy me but my own thoughts; and my thoughts much of the time have been disturbing. I have always been unlike the majority of people. Since I have built up a life to suit my own interests, I have become more and more a specialist, disinterested and remote from the world in general. Most people are interested in a greater variety of subjects, yet in few of the subjects that I find absorbing. This shaking-up has stirred me in a most wholesome way. It has been just what I needed. The unpleasant side of the trip has been beneficial too; for it does no one harm to get tired, to walk too much, to be either too hot or too cold, to go hungry for a few hours and to use what Dr. Carel called the "adaptive functions". If I have become painfully conscious of my mental weaknesses and limitations, I am heartened to see how well my constitution stands up to these tests. My brain is a poor one; inadequately trained; I cannot concentrate for long; I cannot take in more than a few facts at a time; I am unable to remember figures. Perhaps because I am not sufficiently interested, I do not listen carefully to what is being said. I become distracted, and dissipate my thoughts in many directions. Even when travelling for hours in a truck, I am incapable, hard as I try, of thinking along one particular line. In my companions, all the time, I have been most fortunate. I have learnt a deal about good behaviour. Although concessions are made all the while to me by the others, and I am conscious of their intuitive feeling that I am not one of them, I am critical of them when I know they would be charitable towards me. The tolerance shown in the army is remarkable. A man is seldom judged, practically never condemned. There is very little backbiting and malice; and every man is impelled to behave just as well as he can to the community of which he is an organic part. Selfishness is the exception. The only man who behaved unlike the others, who showed up poorly by contrast, was suffering from thyroid trouble, a hospital case of toxic poisoning which caused the mind to react in an unnatural way.

I have not flinched at some of the rough passages, and have enjoyed the idea of seeming to be "a sport", but I have clung to my selfish civilian interests. I have not renounced my home, and have known that soon, God willing, I should be able to return to the life that suited me and to which I was accustomed. Perhaps if I had given up my freedom, once and for all, it would have made some of the delays and setbacks easier for me. There have been many times when I have wished that I could face possible disaster with the same cheerfulness as the others. I have felt physically fitter than when I lived in the big cities; but, perhaps as a result of six months' hard travel, I have recently become rather morbid and introspective.

Kunming, Thursday, May 18th. Maybe the old fire is extinguished in me, but I felt no restlessness at the thought of a week's inactivity. In this large city I feel less stranded than elsewhere. Another asset; after the foul food on the Chinese trains, the cooking here is wonderful; Yunnan hams are a Lucullan treat.

The American hospital is extraordinarily well organised. The buildings are made of solid stuff and well equipped. The day-room, in which the convalescents read their magazines, play cards and paint, is a comfortable and extremely sympathetic place.

In the neighbouring villages threshing was in progress. Old women, with silver balls in their ears and a handkerchief draped to look like a Juliet cap on their head, dumped a mass of wheat in the middle of the road, using any car or cart that passed by to do the work for them. The lotus is grown for its seeds and vegetable roots. Cedar trees, with branches lopped off for fuel, grow to enormous heights and, lining the roads in avenues, remind one of France.

In a corner a group of Shanghai-ites are exchanging news of the people they used to know:

"What's happened to Mrs. Thornton?"

"Oh, she died in thirty-six."

"And her husband?"

"He's in the bag — they've given him the job of distributing the coal in the camp."

"Ha ha, that's bloody funny — he was the managing director of the biggest coal company before the war. I suppose now he's dealing it out by the pound.

And what's happened to that woman who used to wear those huge hats?"

"Oh, Mrs. Wilkinson — they put her husband in the bag, but left her out. It seems they thought her too old to be a nuisance: I don't think she was at all flattered."

Colonel Winters, who has escaped from a Japanese prison, said that sometimes he had been cross-examined for nine hours on end. "But," he said, "they don't torture the English; the Nips are afraid there'd be too much of a row. But if you got ill in prison life was not worth living, for they did not bother about you until you were so ill that they thought you were going to die; only then did they send you to the hospital, as they did not wish to have any deaths in the camp. But the Chinese had a bad time, for the Nips didn't consider there'd be anyone to shout for them. The Chinese came back to their cell beaten up, scarred with bruises and half dead. One favourite torture was to pour a tub full of water down the nose to swell the stomach. Yet most Chinese recovered."

An airmail envelope costs three and six: an ordinary pencil two guineas. Although the value of the Chinese dollar was supposedly fixed five years ago, since foreign supplies have been virtually cut off and the opportunity of underselling locally produced goods has vanished, it has been impossible to keep prices down; and the value of money has decreased as the value of goods has gone up. There is no real shortage of food in most parts of Unoccupied China; the vast bulk of people are better off than before the war. Pasture commands high prices, and the farmers have paid off their mortgages. The poor have a reasonable standard of living at the expense of the salaried *bourgeoisie*. School teachers, professors, students, small government officials, and others of the white collar class are the hardest hit, for their salaries have not been proportionately raised, whereas those of the coolie and artisan have increased at least five hundred times in ratio to the rise in the cost of living. Each city, overcrowded with refugees, has its own price scale. Each seems more expensive than the last. Merchants hoard rice, salt and oil, convinced that prices have not yet reached their zenith. Generally prices are rising at the rate of a thirteen per cent. increase each month, but every new day brings its particular financial shocks. Of all cities, Kunming is considered the most expensive. It is the most fabulous city in the world. Here oranges grow profusely, yet they sell for over eighty dollars apiece — at the official rate a Chinese dollar is worth threepence. Matches here cost twelve dollars a box and, since only one in four Chinese matches is effective, a light for your cigarette costs threepence. Twenty locally rolled cigarettes cost eighty to ninety dollars; a haircut, one hundred and fifty dollars. Sergeant Porter, from Cambridge, who does the catering for his mess, gave me the following current prices:

Pork   ..   .. One hundred and twenty dollars per pound.
Chicken ..   ..One hundred and fifty dollars per pound.
Brown sugar..One hundred and sixty dollars per pound.
Rice   ..   .. Eight hundred and forty dollars per pound.
Butter   ..   .. Seven hundred and fifty dollars per pound (local).
                    Fifteen hundred dollars per pound (tinned).

A fish weighing one and three-quarter pounds, a lunch for four, costs three hundred and seventy dollars, and vegetables for one meal for the same number, eighty-five dollars. Peanut and vegetable oil are used instead of cooking fat, which costs two hundred and twenty dollars.

Nor does one receive value for money. I was lent a mosquito net. In India to-day it could be bought new for four rupees. It was a badly made net, inadequate for any known-sized bed; it was splitting at the seams and dangerously perforated — price, twenty pounds. A visit to the cinema to see a badly scratched Bette Davis in a three-year-old film in a slightly insanitary atmosphere costs two pounds. I was living in circumstances that by none could be considered luxurious; my meals, though simple, cost ten pounds a day; there was a plug, but it didn't work. To bring four buckets of rather muddy water to the bathroom the carriage alone was two pounds. The refuse on the river bank below my balcony encouraged flies and bluebottles, and every night brought its invasions of mosquitoes; the rain poured through my ceiling; yet for the lease of these rat-infested rooms the British Military Mission pays a rental of fifty thousand dollars per month. When the lease is renewed, the landlord wishes to charge four hundred thousand dollars per month. In certain instances prices have increased ten thousand per cent., and amateur mathematicians can work out for themselves the percentage increase of the following:-

A rickshaw ride for one and a half miles formerly cost ten cents — today fifty dollars. People who before paid four dollars fifty cents national currency dollars for their food per month now pay two thousand five hundred.
Gym shoes, formerly seventy-five cents, are now seven hundred dollars.
Mushrooms (admittedly a luxury to the English) formerly ninety cents now cost one hundred dollars for half a pound.

Under the present circumstances money has no significance to the Englishman who remains in China. The pound, before the war when exchanged for Chinese money, bought the equivalent of at least £2 5s.; to-day it is worth two shillings. Although the official rate of exchange is eighty dollars to the pound, in order to ease the financial strain on "official bodies working in the country", a subsidy is granted, whereby the pound is exchanged for one hundred and sixty dollars.

Police force

Boy printer

The American is able to exchange his dollar on the open market, thereby benefiting by an exchange that is five times the rate that the bank would give him at a subsidised rate. But this procedure of using the open market is officially prohibited to the British, a prohibition which baffled the Chinese and added to the discomfiture of the British exile, already punchdrunk with financial blows, who somehow or other must buy the barest necessities. Only when you have something to sell are you told that certain prices have fallen from their peak. It is true that, since quantities of quinine were released on the market, the prices per tablet have decreased. But one tablet of sulphurguanadine (against dysentery) to-day fetches eighty dollars. Anyone with an outdated camera film roll to sell would benefit by fifteen hundred dollars. A gallon of petrol fetches eight hundred dollars; a worn-out motor tyre sixty thousand dollars; an old wireless set between eighty and one hundred and fifty thousand dollars; and an old car is worth literally a million dollars.

Wednesday, May 29th. Awoke to find the skies still grisly, but not too bad for flying. I packed my bag carefully, neatly. Now that I have jettisoned so much it shuts easily. They would ring from the airport, informing me at what time to be ready. But they did not telephone, so I got through to them. They said no aircraft was leaving for Chungking to-day.

Once more that sinking, trapped feeling. I was really at the end of my tether after so many delays. Day after day I had been told I was leaving, and yet I had not moved from the compound. I have become thoroughly stale, unable to do any writing. I returned dismally to my dreary bedroom filled with flies and

mosquitoes; the balcony still flooded with dirty rainwater. I forced myself to write, but with such difficulty! I worked until my eyes ached; ached too much to read. I leant over the balcony watching the life on the river below: a small boy, not more than five years old, was rowing his mother in a heavy barque, the mother busy baling water and shovelling her cargo of sand, dredged from the river's bank.

Three boys came along at great speed in their boat, flanked by flicking, diving cormorants: extraordinary birds with long, thin necks. The birds dived out of sight beneath the green waters, leaving no ripples — a most successful conjuring trick; then they came up again with a silver fish in the mouth; this they swallowed as far as the silver band, which bound the base of their neck, would allow. When the long funnel-neck was filled with fish, the boys hauled the birds out of the river, squeezed the fish out from the bill, and threw the birds back to do more fishing. The haul was remarkably big; the birds were apparently in a desperate state of excitement; and for me too this was the excitement of the day.

The evening was spent in the company of a new arrival — a Scot on his way to Kweilin, poor brute, who talked about the difficulties of stopping the Indians from "scoring a point" instead of taking the war seriously. He seemed keen and said: "It's a great life; I've travelled a thousand miles to-day."

CHAPTER THREE

Return to Chungking

A T last I returned to Chungking. While I had been absent, though nothing had been done, the house, in which I stay had become bigger, more beautiful and incredibly luxurious. I was delighted to be back. Everything looked so appetising. Before, on my arrival from India, I had thought it rather sordid: thus does one get attuned to various degrees of comfort, and accept different standards. It was so pleasant to sit and have tea and talk to Lady S. about all the things I liked. Sir H. was equally sympathetic. He said he noticed I was interested in people, and spent my time exchanging ideas with those whom I liked. In the Diplomatic Service he had not the privilege of liking or disliking.

A relief to be able to discard one's old luggage, and to find a few unexpected, forgotten treasures in the bag left behind. I have become attuned to such poverty that a half-filled cigarette tin, a pot of shaving cream and a fresh shirt are a Crœsus hoard.

Terrific heat: I was awakened at dawn by the telephone. "This is the last day of the Session at which all the provincial governors and cabinet ministers are meeting. Could you come to the Parliament Building by seven o'clock to take photographs of the great occasion?"

Little Professor Chi, sweating from head to foot, having rushed from the airport, was waiting by the roadside for me. Although it was not yet seven o'clock in the morning, the heat was almost annihilating. Dr. Chi kept mopping himself, and like the rabbit in "Alice" muttering repeatedly, "Oh dear, we're late. The Ministers are arriving, the Ministers are arriving."

Armed with blue flashes, we went through the portals of the Parliament Building, only to be stopped at the top of a flight of stairs by a young soldier who demanded to see our military permits. Dr. Kung, the Finance Minister, arrived at this moment and said we could come in with him. But the soldier was adamant. An altercation ensued. Dr. Kung threw his arms in the air. Professor Chi mopped himself anew.

Dr. Kung

"Come and have a little rest," invited Dr. Chi. I had learnt before that this means that there is a serious hitch. Dr. Chi kept muttering under his breath — "There's the Minister of the Interior, oh dear, there's the Minister of Education — of Agriculture."

The lobbies were filled: crowds fanned themselves, drank tea, read newspapers. The written permit arrived simultaneously with the ringing of a bell as everyone went into session. I prowled around clicking my camera, while the proceedings were on. I was asked several times if I understood Chinese; if so, I must "get the hell out". This was a secret session.

The modernistic Assembly Room was dripping with flags and decorated with ornamental trees and a large photograph of Sun Yat Sen. Dr. Kung, presiding, reminded me of Mr. Bevin in appearance. He has humour, a certain charm, but I should imagine he could be cruelly ruthless. Most members seemed to pay little attention to the morning's agenda; they read newspapers. In an interval I had an opportunity to photograph all the Ministers and heads of Yunan. Most of them were so photogenic that it would be impossible to take an uninteresting picture. Some old men were the replicas of paintings of former dynasties, with long straggling beards, fingers like cheese sticks and attenuated drapery of gown.

As we were about to leave the building there was a great clicking of soldiers' feet; bayonets snapped; a concourse of cars; and the Generalissimo came slowly up the stairs, wearing a topee and dark glasses. Off came the topee, off the dark glasses. He acknowledged the deferential nods of a few stragglers. He looked clean, well chiselled and well pressed; perhaps most remarkable, he looked extremely cool. He did not hurry. His face is of a suety texture, with the blunt features of Leon Quartermaine, the English actor. His pate is as carefully shaved as his chin. He was followed by an escort of tough-looking men in uniform, some of whom gestured, with wild flapping of arms and impatient grimaces, at the sentries and others in the lobby to move back. This menacing pantomime let down the tone of the whole entry, and robbed the Generalissimo of much of his dignity. The furtive gesticulating had a gangsterish air; it reminded me of young men in the old days at New York dances, who, getting stuck with an unattractive partner, grimaced or held up a dollar bill behind her back for someone to "cut in".

Fuhtan University, evacuated from Shanghai, is now situated within a hundred miles from Chungking. It was a shock to see the professors, who before the war were great figures in the world of culture and lived in an aura of esteem and luxury, now near destitution. Professors' salaries have not been raised in proportion to the cost of living. To-day our unappetising roadside lunch for two cost three hundred dollars. A professor is paid one thousand dollars a month. He subsists on poor quality rice; he sleeps and works in a prison-like cell, with no one to tend him. He possesses no furniture except perhaps a board propped on two dictionaries as a bed, and a case with shelves for the volumes salvaged from his former life. In accordance with the "Oil Thrift" movement, the lamp must be put out early at night. Living like peasants are the great specialists and experts on French literature or European philosophy; men who have been editors of scientific magazines, who have been the pivot of intellectual life and thought, are stranded here without money for cigarettes, some of them suffering from foot-rot so that they are unable to walk, and others from disease caused by under-nourishment and lack of baths. Yet they remain astoundingly cheerful and full of verve. Dr. Liang entertained us with fascinating anecdotes about Paul Valéry and his other friends; and he gave us a glass of tiger-bone wine, a potent and invigorating drink. Another professor talked of Dryden and Maugham with a combination of charm of manner, authority and humility. In the room next door his sister was working, but when called, she would not appear because she had not on her best dress, and did not wish to be seen looking like a servant. Dr. Young was an authority on contemporary English poets, and quoted Empson and Auden. He was at the moment translating into English the poems of Dr. Liu, not because he considered them good poems, but "because he is a friend of mine". He told us how Dr. Liu is of the old school, is accepted by the Government and writes about poetic generals. Dr. Liu publishes one book of poems per month. This is not considered excessive. These professors were touchingly benign and tolerant; yet in spite of their intellectual manner and their charm, it was occasionally impossible for them to rise above their present surroundings, not to be contaminated in some way by this squalor caused by lack of money. Even if they were fitted to earn their living by any other means, it would be considered degrading for them to take to trade.

One of the few benefits the enemy's advance has forced upon the extremely conservative population of China (eighty per cent. of whom are an agricultural people) is an increased knowledge of their own country. Before the war there were not many Chinese who travelled more than a few miles from the orbit of their family; Chinese life was largely provincial. In many instances these migrations will be permanent. Thus the racial stock will be revitalised by the new arrivals and infusion of fresh blood.

"Have you slept enough?" This was a nice way of being called by my host. The morning toilet was carried out in a most public way; a basin of water was put on the one table in his wife's bedroom. It seems that in China there is no question of "retiring" for the night; no secrecy surrounds the hours of rest; one merely flops down on the floor, wrapped in a rug, for an interval of repose, then, on waking, continues as before. In moments of tiredness I become as intolerant as any Blimp. I found the freedom of behaviour or, according to Western standards, the lack of manners, sometimes very disagreeable, particularly when, as often happens, Chinese customs and manners are acquired in exaggerated forms by Englishmen. Certain types of cultured Englishmen, in a determination to "go native" with a vengeance, sigh, yawn, moan, sing, gurk and spit with such a determination, to show their lack of inhibition, that the effect was to make me cussedly genteel. Incidently, I found it strange that English people in China should refer to English cooking as "foreign food".

Even to-day the old University town of Chengtu possesses a great Mission life. The various compounds of granite-coloured brick, with dragon roofs, are swarming with benevolent elderly Canadians and their grey-haired wives with large mouths and pince-nez. Good work is done by these enthusiasts. In spite of the economic conditions that prevail throughout China, the

Students at archery

Boy scouts

exiles still manage to lead an extremely pleasant life, existing in what struck me as comparative luxury. An enormous amount of entertaining seemed to be done. One lady, with a voice like a flint, told me she seldom sat down to any meal with less than a dozen guests.

My days were spent photographing. Long, Low, Wong and I started out early visiting the leading citizens, the Provincial Governor, the Minister of Foreign Affairs, the Presidents of Universities and the Head of the Fire Station. The light was brilliant, and I welcomed the opportunity of polishing off an enormous number of pictures. By the end of one day I had clicked my shutter at every sort of type, from the dentist to the co-operatives, at scenes of university life in the campus, dormitories, libraries; at the sports; at boxing matches and shops heaped with sandals bearing coloured bobbles, like brilliant flowers; at the baskets of ripe peaches, pretty porcelain jars, blue and white; and at idyllic scenes under the hanging foliage of pepper and willow trees that gave me, perhaps for the first time, an impression of what once I imagined China to be. By the end of my first day I had managed to expose over one hundred and fifty pictures. I kept up this average for several days. On the morrow, Dr. Wilsford showed us over the Canadian Mission Hospital of which he is in charge.

In the huge wards there were soldiers with broken limbs, old men and children — some of the children extremely moving, for example a child transfixed with weakness, in a pose of almost incredible beauty. Would-be helpful nurses tried hurriedly to kill the picture before me by their usual maddening "tidying-up" and "straightening" of patients' clothes. A young Chinese soldier was wheeled in, in a rickshaw covered with blood. Five minutes later, his head covered with a wad on which ether was being sprinkled, he was lying on the operating table. His left arm was almost severed, the hand lying limp, the pointed fingers gesticulating for the last time. After we had visited various floors of the hospital, we returned to the theatre to find the amputation had taken place. The red stump was being sewn up; the tendons clipped with cotton. Half the young man's livelihood had gone; for although he had received his injuries at the arsenal (his arm caught in a machine) he would receive little, if any, pension.

At the Chengtu Military Academy, General Wan Yal Hwan arranged a tremendous practice demonstration for the Generalissimo's forthcoming visit, with the march past of thousands of troops, cavalry, infantry, girl guides and the smallest boy scouts. By the end of the day, with people making suggestions for pictures almost incessantly — "Take this arbour" — "Take this platoon" — "Do these wrinkles interest you?" — my temper grew jagged. All were well meant — but it is fatiguing to explain that I cannot take anything except the subjects I know come within the orbit of my camera. By the end of the day

I find my voice goes: I enunciate very clearly in a pale but exasperated invalid's voice. This is a new sign of approaching age.

At the next door house, the European colony had turned up in full force for a wedding. The festivities were almost over when we arrived. The Chinese bride, born in Canada, her hair in permanent curls, had substituted her pink satin dress for the "going-away" print. The twelve-year-old son of the Canadians in whose house the reception was given was overtired, tough and spoilt — a horrible combination. There were tempers, tears, and father took sonny up to bed for a well-deserved hiding. The flowers were wilting; the cake crumbling. Everyone looked a bit harassed, except the bridegroom, who leapt over a flower-bed at the approach of his bride in her travelling costume: a touching and gallant piece of athletics. Post-mortem — "The cake turned out well after all — You don't mind do you? But we stole your raisins!"

Friday, June 9th, Chungking. Overcast sky, damp exhausting heat, the activity of the last days in such a climate has taken its toll. I feel utterly limp. The S.'s returned for late luncheon, both pretty jaded after a gruelling morning's work. The Japs are doing only too well; a big evacuation has taken place. Missionaries turn up unexpectedly by the score: one Canadian woman escaped from behind the Jap lines disguised as a Chinese peasant, some of her orphans with her, but most of the others had gone back to their relations. One of the missionaries described the last night in the Mission. "Just as we were turning in, we heard shouts outside. It was the Tidmans! With Imogene, Timothy and Aunt Lottie. Somehow we managed, but we were eleven! So we overlapped a bit. Mr. Tompkins slept in with Mr. Webster; and we all piled in the B.M.M. truck next morning." Gloomy accounts of the Chinese resistance. It is feared the Japs will be in Changsha to-morrow . . . . We were all so tired at the end of the evening that Sir H. said, "It's lazy not to get up and go to bed."

Air-raid sirens shrieked, and lanterns of different colours were hoisted to give warning. Excited shouts from the rabbit warrens of the town. When the raid is serious people take as many of their possessions as possible and go to the dugouts in the rocks, which are commodious enough to shelter the entire population of nearly a million. Nowadays it is calculated that only one person is killed for every three bombs that fall. To-night the mountain roads were flanked with humanity awaiting the final signal to retreat into the caves. Everyone with cars takes to the road, and the exodus stretches for miles into the country. A great deal of valuable fuel is wasted.

What greater tribute can one pay the widow of Dr. Sun Yat Sen,

Madame Sun Yat Sen

than to say that in present-day China she is poor? She is the most popular woman in Chungking; kindly, sincere, courageous and known to have the welfare of China at heart. In a country where to be outspoken is sometimes dangerous, she does not hide her disappointment at the distance she believes the Government has travelled from the principles laid down by her husband, the Father of the Republic.

This gallant, rather tragic, little figure is continuously breaking into laughter. She screws up her face, like a baby about to cry, with a mirth that is alternately childlike and hearty. She laughs in answer to a compliment, laughs as a lament, laughs as a means of expressing agreement and understanding when, even for her, to be more precise would be unwise. She is almost peasant-like in her intuitive simplicity. When I suggested a pose with clasped hands for a drawing I wished to make of her, she grimaced as if tasting a sour fruit and said: "Oh no, Sir Cecil, it is not good for me; it is not suitable." Instinctively she knows what is correct for her, her limitations, her potentialities. She looks like Mrs. Noah; her gestures are slightly masculine, her fingers fattish and pointed; her diminutive feet hang uselessly like a doll's, not long enough to touch the floor. She is businesslike, frank and direct. She lives in a small gimcrack villa, immaculately swept and garnished, where the flowers, sent by faithful friends who possess small patches of garden, are plumped into metal shell-cases and a variety of pots. Thence she sallies forth, and learns perhaps more of the public opinion in Chungking than any other member of her family.

▨▨▨▨▨▨ Local news is bad; it seems probable that the Japs may cut China in two and capture all of the rest of Free China. They could even concentrate on stopping our supplies over the Hump. No one is visibly panicky; for so long the worst has been expected; but pleasant surprises sometimes belie the gloomiest portents. Nevertheless, everyone is secretly worried as to how the various armies will meet the three Jap thrusts. Some armies fight with zeal, others may not: much depends upon the generals on the spot, on transport problems and on reinforcements.

▨▨▨▨▨▨ There is even talk of the possibility of the Japs taking Chungking and of the Central Government splitting. Certain local war lords have been very frank with the Americans as to the gravity of the present situation. Why? Is it an attempt to get even more help from the U.S. Army, based on the knowledge that they would not be likely to clear out of China now, when they have already done so much? The Americans wish to give the Chinese help; but it is said they do not intend to send an army to withstand a possible attack from Indo-China.

▨▨▨▨▨▨ Dinner at the K.C. Wu's. He is the Mayor of Chungking* and one of the most highly thought of young men in China to-day. To-night he was brilliant, with apt quotations from Shakespeare and other poets, of which few of the English present knew the source. The hostess was enchanting. In turquoise blue, with rouge on her cheeks, she looked sixteen, though she has three large children. She showed us some of her paintings. She specialises in the "flower-insect family," studies sprays of peach-blossom, then paints her pictures from memory. To me her technique seemed quite formed and sure, but she must continue to develop strength before tackling an orchid. This, it appears, is the most difficult of all flowers to interpret in the Chinese idiom, for the spontaneous strokes necessary demand great vigour. We studied various forms of calligraphy, and tried to learn why one scroll was better than another.

Cooking at the Wu's is acknowledged the best in Chungking. I did not know before how delicious Chinese cooking could be. There was not too much of it; the wine was not disagreeable; and there was just enough toasting to put everyone in good spirits without turning the party into a debauch.

▨▨▨▨▨▨ I wanted to photograph war-orphans; but I found myself at a Nursery School for the children of Government officials who are too badly off to afford nurses. "Why have I not been sent to see the war orphans?" At first I was told I *had* photographed them. After denying that emphatically many times, I learn-

*He has since become Vice Minister of Foreign Affairs.

A.R.P. fireman

Sweetmeat seller

ed that "they" did not wish the orphans to be photographed. This, it appears, was a punishment for the fact that I was alleged to have photographed the New Life Building without permission. Before I could be allowed the privilege of taking a photograph, it seemed that the orphans' faces had to be washed and made-up. A woman friend told me she had discovered that there are about a dozen orphans, who are farmed out for different official visits; that when she went to some hostel with Mrs. Chiang she recognised the same brat serving tea whom she had seen previously at two other functions.

Carton de Wiart. One of the historical personalities of this war — he negotiated the Italian Armistice — and a hero of the last, General Carton de Wiart arrived in Chungking at this time as Churchill's Chinese right ear.

Although no English blood runs in his veins, his appearance and manner are those of the traditional English warrior. With one eye, one arm, the Victoria Cross, and, he says, very few brains, he is an adventurer in the grand manner. With his Cyrano-like nose, his one remaining eye and his matchboard body, he is as dashing as the blade of a sword.

General Carton de Wiart

The opinion was expressed that the General had not the necessary political knowledge for the job he was to hold. Within a few days of his arrival it was admitted that he said things frankly and boldly that politicians might be chary of voicing. Legends were soon circulated of the General's fiery brilliance, wit, courtier-like gallantry, annihilating charm and almost ungovernable temper. If a sentry were to hold up the General on the threshold of the Generalissimo's house, the General's complexion might become purple-brown. One of his entourage admitted that the General is not easy to work with, but proudly added: "You're not given the V.C. for knitting. He's of a stuff young men aren't made of to-day."

General Carton considers as his home every place he stays in for more than a few weeks. (He went to Poland for a holiday and remained twenty years.) Now China has become home to him.

"Why the delay, Chi? We haven't rushed here at this early hour of the morning to wait half an hour outside an office. Let the manager come and join us as soon as he arrives. I'm going to take pictures of that market there."

Mr. Chi, wearing the armband of the Chinese Ministry of Information, was loath to conduct me to the market. I was insistent. "I hope no one will interfere with us," he hinted. This terror is typical of all minor officials. Later, Mr. Chi was superseded by a Mr. Li. We crossed the Yangtse river. The morning was spent taking photographs in the Navy Factory and Dockyards, where most of the important work is done in caves blasted in the rocks, safe from bombing. The activity of the dockyards was impressive — boys sawing pine planks in a frenzied trance, coolies lifting enormous weights with only the minimum pause for rest. Some criminals were working under the eyes of the Military; they had shaven heads with a tuft of black hair like a pompom on the top. They looked soured-up and brutal, and pretty ugly.

At the cotton mill which we later visited, hundreds of tissue-paper-skinned girls were working, their black satin hair grey with flying wisps of cotton. I judged how nervously tired I was from the fact that, if anyone came round to fuss about my pictures, I was inclined to be ungenerous and, when anyone moved during a time-exposure, almost shouted my head off with fury.

The morning was wet and sticky, and I poured with sweat like a sponge; but I enjoyed travelling in the ferry boats and sampans, and had my first experience of a sedan chair ride. This seems to be the ultimate luxury. By evening, having photographed a cigarette factory, the hideous gothic Cathedral, the Police Station, an Admiral and the Communist H.Q., and having had to change my soused clothes three times, I felt it would be madness ever to click the trigger again.

▓▓▓▓▓ *Wednesday, June 21st. The Return Journey. Dawn Departure.* Still raining. Our pavilion in a cloud. Visibility zero. Shu and Wong, the delightful servants, waved good-bye. I left the dark little house, feeling I would probably return there for breakfast after a lengthy misunderstanding at the airport. The daylight strengthened, but the dangerously close mountains remained invisible. We waited, in the rain, for six hours before we heard that the aircraft which was to take us on our long journey was still stranded at Chengtu, but would be here within an hour.

A friend who had come to bid me farewell spent the time discussing the predicament of China to-day. He said he feared that the only possible solution lay in revolution: too many of the country's leaders were unscrupulous opportunists. The Chinese are greedy; they always want more: never know when to stop. "Aid to China" should not be given in sums of money that lose their value at the present rate of exchange, but in medicine and clothes, to be distributed for specific objects through reliable sources. We must continue to be friends with China, but a different sociological attitude must be adopted, and the picture of Gallant China with its back to the wall must be discarded for a more realistic one. "We should try," my friend continued, "to see other people's points of view. It does not hurt us to employ Chinese technique. When I sack a Chinese clerk, I call him in for a long talk. I ask him if he does not feel he is wasting his time in the office. Couldn't he be of more use to China elsewhere? Why doesn't he think about that? By degrees, members of the family come in to thank me for the advice. They decide the clerk could certainly be of more use to China elsewhere. Although they know it's a sack no one is hurt," my friend explained. "A present is given to me, by one of the family in recognition of my kindness; the clerk leaves; my other Chinese clerks remain. But suppose I lost my patience one morning, and sacked a delinquent clerk on the spot! All the other clerks would leave in sympathy with the outcast. It is necessary to respect the Chinese way of behaviour. Never get impatient; never give them a time-limit. If you say, 'everything must be ready in three hours,' they will spend all their time wondering why you said 'three hours' and not 'four' or 'two'."

We looked up at where the mountains would be visible, if they were not hidden in rain-clouds.

"Anyone who's been to China is considered an expert, you know," my friend continued. "What do you feel as the result of your trip?"

I had arrived in abysmal ignorance of the country, but with the highest expectations. I discovered China in 1944 to be unlike all preconceived impressions. I was appalled by the poverty of the ordinary inhabitant of the most populous country on earth. From bamboo hovel to the paddy fields and back is the existence of millions — with no light to read by — with no distractions but periodic disaster. It seems the Chinese labourer is always being exploited. His history is a repetition of being ground down, badly led, and then abandoned to his doom.

I admit to neither speaking, reading nor understanding ten words of Chinese; my impressions may have been gleaned from unauthentic gossip; but even a stranger, travelling in as many out-of-the-way places as I had, could not fail, every now and again, to receive a true picture. Neither can I be accused of prejudice. Whenever, at first, I came across a European whom I found to be critical, I thought that here was another example of the provincial judging everything from the standpoint of his hearth. But it did not take me many weeks to realise, when many allowances are made, that conditions are often worse than they need be, and that there must be some justification for the serious accusations that one hears about the corruption, dishonesty and "squeeze" employed in the running of the country and the conduct of the war. I had visited China at perhaps its darkest period, after seven years of war. I saw the country in its least flattering aspect. In peacetime a nation gives only a passive display of its characteristics, but in war, while it shows its spirit, it also reveals its faults. At the moment, the Chinese have few opportunities of making progress in constitutional government; the National Military Council directs all party, political and military affairs; the Central Government has recourse to adopt Supreme Authority; a rigid censorship prevents natural freedom of expression.

Modern China has been robbed of all its graceful arabesques, has been reduced to essentials, to the lowest common denominator. From the visual point of view the life of the common people appears to be more medieval than Ming. The sturdy, squat peasant-folk engaged in incessant toil have less connection with the *chinoiseries* of Chippendale or Boucher than with the visions of an orientalised Bruegel or Bosch. Possibly some of the more prosperous villagers might have been painted by a Chinese Le Nain; but the Frenchman's peasants, at the end of their day's work, enjoyed a flagon of wine. Not so the Chinese, who refreshes and stimulates himself with a cup of hot water. The poorest in England and America possess their pot of geranium or cactus at the window; the Chinese mud hut is often without the privacy of a door, and certainly boasts no sill. China's stubborn resistance to a merciless and highly mechanised foe has won her lasting praise. The army, with little equipment and the poorest supplies, has faced a powerful enemy with optimistic tenacity and stubborn endurance. One million and a half Japanese soldiers are still tied up, if not actively engaged in battle. Even so, there are those who now consider China's hand has been overplayed by certain of her country's emissaries, and that the inevitable swing-back will be cruel; the golden honeymoon may so soon be

Provincial governor's wife

Chinese mask

followed by divorce proceedings, and the ripping of the veil is always a painful process.

Yet how deserving is the ordinary Chinese, of whom fifty millions have been made refugees by the Japanese advance! Cheerful and hardworking, he does his job always with something near to artistry. He carries two trees of bamboo over his shoulder with gaiety and a perfection of balance; he disperses the weight of the great load with wonderful ingenuity. To watch him at work in the fields is to marvel at a technique perfected through thousands of years. He utilises everything nature provides, with the utmost virtuosity. He lights the natural gases from the earth, using them for his stove. At the salt mines, he unlooses a long cylinder thirty feet below the ground, winds it up again to the surface filled with brine, which he then cooks, dries, cleans and converts into large lumps of salt. He hoards his own excreta to fertilise his fields. He wastes nothing. To make their contribution in the fight against oppression, even the women, whose place was always the home, have taken up pick and spade to build new roads for front-line supplies.

I had come across many delightful Chinese. There was, for example, the man running a factory who had been, among other things, a mechanic, a sailor and a coolie. He had organised the welfare of his workers, their dormitories, canteens and First Aid rooms, with the same enthusiasm that he had showed in inventing ingenious devices for replacing rare goods and saving labour. There was Dr. Yen, the galvanic little managing director of a factory where, in spite of officials who try to impede his efforts, he succeeds in making all sorts of wireless and radio equipment. In this country, where machinery seems to be considered something that must forthwith be broken, his achievement appeared all the more remarkable. Dr. Yen was in charge of over a thousand workers who, out of old oil drums, scrap paper and general wastage, create, perhaps, the only first-class and perfect newly-made objects I had seen made since my arrival. Fourteen-year-old students were learning to make the transmitters that the Chindits use in the jungle. Everything was checked and cross-checked; here were no broken springs, chipped edges and cracked crockery. Dr. Yen had shown what China is capable of achieving . . . .

During our conversation the weather became worse. The rain quivered as in an old Bioscope film. No chance of the clouds dispersing. Though we could not see it, eventually we heard our aircraft as it circled above the mountains. Suddenly a pale grey shadow appeared through the mist, only fifty feet from the landing strip, and the vast machine skimmed down through the wires stretching between the gorges. A torrential splash, and the machine landed dead straight on the runway. At last it seemed we were leaving. I shook my

friend by the hand. "After all," he said, "anything you say of China is true —
it's so large a country — good-bye."

Through pouring rain I made towards the aircraft. I tried to take my mind
off my terror by eating some cake, but it turned to saw-dust in my mouth. In
ten minutes we climbed above the storm-clouds and emerged in brilliant sunshine over harsh, clear mountains . . . . .

When at last we landed, the atmosphere was dry, peppery and spiced. It
seemed wonderful to be in India again. I was in holiday mood and tasted all the
joys of recovered freedom.

CHAPTER FOUR

The Journey Back

I REMAINED a few weeks in India, working to instructions from Bloomsbury. Then the monsoon burst with dramatic violence. Much of the countryside was flooded; photography became impossible; and I was told that, if transport were available, I could fly home *via* the United States. Full of excitement at the idea of returning to New York after these last years, I started out on my return journey. At Karachi we waited. The rains had submerged a whole area of the Air Station. So many tents had been flooded that, for many of us stranded on the flying field, there was no accommodation. We sat around, hoping that maybe a cot in a corridor would become available and we could lie down to sleep. Meanwhile the scene was extraordinary; the asphalt a torrent; Indians wading up to their knees; the jeeps driving through waves of café-au-lait; the planes themselves, like enormous silver flying-fish, marooned on dunes or floating on a sea.

We hung around corridors; for we must be available. After a few days, the weather improved and at last an aircraft took off. Now that there was a chance that we, too, might leave, we were weighed; we filled in forms; we were "briefed" in case of "ditching." A lecture was given telling us what to do if we came down in the sea. We were to appoint a captain for each dinghy, and to abide by everything he said. We must not be extravagant with our water ration, we would not know for how long we might need it: we should clean our teeth in it, swill it around the mouth for a long time before eventually gulping it down. We must never become despondent, for surely help would come. It was worth going where we were going, said the American, "for there's a nice cool drink awaiting you. And now," he continued, "about Mae Wests — put the thing on just like a halter (you'll excuse any reference to a horse). But — one vital thing — leave plenty of room to spare under the arms and crutch, for when the thing inflates it becomes much tighter, and might damage you. You don't want to take any risks; you don't want to arrive where you're going with anything wrong with the crutch." I reflected that, should we have to take to a dinghy, I should be utterly incapable of using the radio or any of the mechanical gadgets with which we were supplied . . . .

After days of waiting the word "go" was given. About two dozen of us trooped into a vast D.C. 46. My fellow travellers were all Americans, most of them Merill's Marauders; one nice chap from Alabama, with a tremendous drawl, was going home, having flown fifty times over the Hump. The take-off on the still waterlogged runway was spectacular; but we climbed into the air and settled down on the first part of our journey. From Aden we crossed Africa to Ascension Island, then to Brazil, Trinidad and Miami. If we were lucky, our goal should be reached within a week.

But we were not lucky. After flying over the sea for two hours we were directed to return; the weather had "closed in at Missouri". We returned to our starting-point — to the same flooded station, to the same food, the same impossibility of escape to the town to sight-see or to go to a movie; for we were again to be "at readiness" to leave at a minute's notice. Again we did all the things that we hoped we had done for the last time; filling in more forms, getting cards for billeting, tickets for meals; and again the weather deteriorated.

Finally, after another roll-call, we trooped back into our seats in the plane. We were locked in. The pilot took up his position for the run, and there he remained. The lights in our compartment were switched off and on, on and off. Eventually he taxied back whence we had started. The pilot explained that the "feathering" of the air-screws did not work. We trooped out again, hung around, then into the aircraft again. Once more a false alarm; the pilot said "Missouri weather" had again "closed-down". We had had three false starts. Now I went to an available cot, rather thankful not to have to spend the night in the aircraft. One good night's sleep would help; but it was not to be. Ten minutes after I was undressed, word came that, after all, we were off; and this time it was final.

We started. It was dark. The floor of the aircraft was covered with bodies sprawled out on every available inch of space. At Aden, "the Vestibule of the Orient", we said good-bye to the chalky and sultry whiteness of India. Now below us was Africa, with palm trees, mud, marabouts and camels.

The noise of the aircraft makes one feel high strung, and tears stream when one reads an emotional book. It is curious how, in spite of the tremendous noise of the four engines, one hears every additional noise — the click of a playing-card slammed down, the metal ping as someone hits his head against the ceiling of the fuselage, the nasal voices of the passengers shouting to one another. I drifted into a sort of coma; no day had any particular beginning or end. We slept in the aircraft at all times of day and night. We landed at various anonymous-looking American airports scattered about Africa, to be bustled into lorries, to drink a wonderful cup of coffee in the Mess, and, in double quick time, be herded back into the aircraft.

After a day's flight in a sunny sky, with sufficient clouds to make us bump around a lot, some of the passengers were sick. I contracted a cold; a generator burnt itself out in the aircraft, and we were delayed. A padré from Utah said this was a blessing, as most of the boys were getting headaches; they could now have a night's sleep. It was a help to get the long growth of beard off one's face, and the coating off one's teeth.

"This beats me," remarked the fastidious captain from Alabama, as he laid down his fork and lumbered off from breakfast. Nor did any of the others do more than pick at the imitation waffles.

The Marauders talked about their life in the jungle. One of them re-enacted, in graphic mime, an unexpected encounter with a Jap, who poked his head around a tree only five yards away. The Jap's rifle was hanging upside down under his rain-coat. "It would take him half an hour to get it into position, so he just smiled at me while I threw a grenade at him."

These youths had out-walked their Mussouri mules; the animals fell flat on their stomachs, with outstretched legs — "then we had to shoot 'em, and before leaving, we'd cut off a lump of flesh and cook it later. It was good enough until someone mentioned that we were eating horseflesh; then I'd have to spit it out, and later start over again."

At night, if a bird whistled, a monkey screamed or the slightest sound was made, they were all wide awake. They never expected more than four hours of sleep; the first thing to do each morning, before eating, was to pack belongings, to be able to take off at a second's notice. Each man had his story to tell. One young man seemed slightly jittery; he confided that the sight of some of his friends bayoneted by the Japs had left an indelible mark upon him. He had left his buddy in a trench for only a few moments; when he came back, "he saw something he didn't like seeing". "My buddy had been bayoneted in the chest, and he hadn't a shirt on." He seemed quite cynical about the people at home. "They are not interested in us out there, they are too busy making fifteen dollars a day; they can't be bothered with the war in Burma — it's too remote — they are making the machines and that's enough for them."

Most of these chaps were still yellow-complexioned as a result of the Atapane they take against malaria. I could not understand the arguments and shop-talk that the pilots maintain: their conversation was altogether too technical, and made me feel utterly useless.

We took off. Landed. Took off again. I had no idea of the time: once I calculated it would be about four o'clock in the afternoon, and discovered it was ten-thirty in the morning. Sometimes we seemed to endure three nights in one. For instance, after an early dinner at Karno, I had gone into the deepest sleep, to be awakened five hours later. We took off in the darkness; and again I slept. After another four hours, we arrived in the dark at Accra, and again I went to sleep; this time a desperate dejected sleep, worn out by the incessant wakings and interruptions. Eventually we arrived at the great West African terminal for America. We had achieved half our journey. Here we changed planes, and here we might wait several days — nobody knew exactly how long. I enjoyed watching the Americans shaving, washing, dressing with such ease and simplicity. They are without inhibitions, shyness or modesty; they walk about naked; their latrines are communal and are used as meccas for gossip; if there should be a door they will never shut it. They live in their shop window, letting all the world see their customs, their fears and their hustle. The pilots laughed among each other; one said, "I always pray at the take-off." Another added blithely: "I'm sick of this war, sick of flying, I want to get back to make some money." They are the least greedy people in the world, their food possesses little fattening value and their sunburnt flanks are as flat as a terrier's. They are "machine-made" in their mental neatness and physical precision. The clothes they wear never really become part of them: they do not seem to contaminate the gum they chew. I enjoy their luxury; their clothes are perpetually being sent to the laundry; they are for ever buying new garments and presents. They are all very bejewelled, with enormous signet rings on both hands. Why is it that one always sees the American G.I. at the moment he takes his first puff at a cigarette — the British Tommy when he is sucking at a discoloured fag end?

Now for the last hop. We flew seven hours through the night, and then, in the early morning sunlight, saw Ascension Island below. The British gave up the idea of ever being able to make this into a landing base, but the American engineers, after dynamiting thousands of tons of rock, have succeeded in manufacturing a wonderful artificial runway. It was a perfect day, with brilliant sun and ultramarine sea. Even so, I felt sorry for the lonely G.I.'s based on this forlorn island, where not a blade of grass grows. They came out to gossip with us during our breakfast and refuelling interval. Another seven-hour hop; the sun moved from one side of the clouds to the other. After covering two thousand five hundred miles we arrived at Natal; an enormous airport, again wonderfully engineered by the Americans, with white starched décolleté sailors and every sort of pilot, including R.A.F. and Brazilians. Although the airport is one hundred per cent. American, a little of Brazil had infiltrated itself: the car driver wore a suit of ice-cream pink, the waiters spoke Portuguese and the coffee was exceptionally good. We lined up in queues for cafeteria meals, bought things from the P.X. One pilot told me he had spent three hundred dollars on trash gifts.

Belem consisted, for us, merely of a compound where Americans behaved like Americans, having shower-baths, going to the movies and spending the minimum time over meals; the trees tropical, the temperature breathless, no air, a huge moon. Again we started off. Although my memory is hazy, I do not think we called anywhere after Puerto Rico. These names sound romantic, but the landings are impersonal: we merely circled a field, our ears buzzed and hurt, and we "b'rumped" down. The aircraft became an oven of heat before we could get out for a queue and a sandwich, presently returning to the furnace for the next take-off.

The last five hours, before Miami, were almost unendurable. I was too excited to concentrate on any book. I looked out of the window at the sea and sky-scapes: some of these were incredibly beautiful — of diverse blues, or of pale greens with yellow and apricot streaks. The calm sea was like plate glass; one could see to the bottom: islands of rock, as we approached Florida, had remarkable Leonardesque character — a strange, unearthly scene. We bumped as we flew through mountainous snowy clouds lit by the evening sun.

At last the twinkling lights. "Oh boy," said a passenger. "I haven't seen anything so good as that for years!" But the freedom of arrival did not start as soon as we landed: many more queues, an exigent customs and a short lecture, which impressed me a good deal:

"Now many of you chaps have seen extraordinary things and your families will want to hear about them. Don't be unduly secretive. Tell them the names of places that have appeared in the news; but if you've made an escape, and others are likely to try to get away by the same means, don't tell your closest friend, because doubtless she has a friend who has a friend who writes radio scripts. And, fellows, one other thing I ask you — Don't criticise your allies. It doesn't help any, and there's plenty of time for that after the war."

I was told I could fly on to New York directly, but this was not to be. My papers were not valid for an army plane. I must wait here. I longed for the luxury of a Miami hotel and escape from the Mess atmosphere of which I had lately had so much. But I discovered that the big hotels were all taken over by the Navy, and the places to which the taxi-driver took me for a night's rest were not very savoury. Even here, with my unshaven chin and hobo clothes, I was recognised as a delinquent, and aroused suspicion at the desk of several "family hotels". I was so over-tired that I may have been slightly hysterical: I was certainly very captious: absurd scenes took place. A negro, escorting me up to an oven in an establishment smelling of old armpits, asked, "Are you French?"

"Why?" I snapped.

"'Cos Mister there are some French people in 'dis hotel who want to talk to *anyone* who can speak French."

"Well, I don't want to speak to anyone in this hotel." And in a flash I was out of it.

At another hostelry, one old man said: "Put down your baggage, buddy." After which another, farther down the hall, asked me in reply to my query for a room: "Have you no luggage?"

The Dallas Park was my refuge for the night. "No, no papers here. No breakfasts served in the hotel." This was not the America I had known. Old forgotten men, looking like Uncle Sam, had come out to be lobby boys or very jerkily work the lift. There was a great shortage of messengers and servants; but, in comparison with England, the shops were still opulent. The news-stands were piled with hundreds of copies of hundreds of magazines, and the cafeterias were plenty itself.

▭▭▭▭ I arrived at dawn in New York, and received my first impression of summer. For, in spite of sunshine and heat, summer does not seem to exist in the Orient. In the small gardens of those ugly wooden shacks that one passes on the way from La Guardia Airfield, heavily scented stocks and lush trailers were growing. But summer was already rather faded. New York was shrouded in the unbecoming haze, lightless and murky, of the hottest August she had known for many years. The city was beginning to wake up; the streets were still empty but for the news sellers; in the gargantuan honeycomb apartment blocks, radios were playing "setting-up exercises".

I arrived at the hotel in which I had spent so many winters. A strange face regarded me from the reception desk. Nevertheless there was a room for me. I was curiously excited, yet shy. Maybe this unaccustomed and somewhat overwhelming humility was due to fatigue. I felt particularly self-conscious when I ventured out into the streets. On arriving at a familiar restaurant for lunch, I was suddenly conscious of all that had happened since I was in New York last. Many changes had taken place; many friends would never return; so much time had gone by. The restaurant had been redecorated, and the fashionable women were wearing new fashions, enormous hats like platters strewn with flowers. I hung back as if suddenly I had become very old, as if too much had happened while I had been away . . . . Life had gone on. Had the elderly Rip lost his touch? I was the victim of a bout of self-pity. If I felt like this, how would they react — the prisoners of war, the men from the jungle, men from a hundred isolated outposts? After years of separation from the life they knew, how could they hope to pick up, when they returned home, a thread of continuity?

I had forgotten much of my past existence in New York. Little by little, old memories, oddly in contrast with my experiences of the last five years, came creeping back again. I had that cold drink that we had all promised ourselves. Before long I was once again caught up in the maelstrom.

Ashcombe, 1945.

Chinese Album

To
CLARISSA
With Love

Foreword

AN alarum clock would call us at four o'clock in the morning. The resilient floorboards of the Chinese hostel cracked as we got dressed, shaved, packed, and as we rolled up the bedding: breakfast of rice and tea: then the company would assemble while the lorry was piled with mountains of baggage. Eventually, after many delays, we would start off on the long day's journey, banging and bouncing over potholes and boulders, semi-circling through winding mountain passes. For weeks on end, we travelled into the heart of unoccupied China towards the front lines of war. There were many compensations for the discomforts, squalors and disappointments. I have returned with thousands of photographs that are so halcyon of aspect that I can hardly realize that, at many times I was prompted to quote Virgil:

> One day I shall be happier looking back on this day.

The wild rose, pummelo and tong trees in flower against a stage backcloth of blue mountains and torrential waterfalls, like strips of glass hanging from the cascading forests of bamboo, made a strangely idyllic setting for the undiminishing and almost frenzied labours of the Chinese people fighting for existence. In the fields they tread large wheels and defy the laws of gravity by driving the water uphill: their bodies are bent double as they weed in the rice swamps, or, like stylized dancers, they stamp down the rice shoots into the bog of the paddy fields, their thigh and calf muscles as developed as a boxer's. Some old men cut green stuff from the roadsides and carry home mountainsides in baskets: others manure the sugar canes: old women, with bound feet — distorted little trotters — hobble along with a whisk of bamboo directing their families of geese.

As in England, in China one can usually see the end of the lane ahead, and along the narrowly circuitous paths the carrier coolies proceed astonishingly quickly in their purgatory of almost unabating toil. Their burdens of rice, salt, coal or lead are almost Herculean. Pigs are strapped upside-down and are wheeled to market, or carried for twenty miles from the shoulder yoke so that they shall not lose weight en route; their supplicating feet, folded back neatly, contribute to the picture of poignant helplessness.

Among the photographs I have selected here, you will see a variety of people working out their God-appointed destiny with deft hands and a patience that is touching: the spinners of silk, the sweetmeat vendors, the gymnasts or the employees in the cigarette factory: you may see the firemen in their brass helmets or Aladdin hats of black and gold straw, and, behind the scenes of the theatre the wonderful head-dresses and theatrical clothes that, amid the turmoil and dirt, are treated as reverently as ecclesiastical vestments.

Perhaps from scrutinizing these pictures you may be able to recognize the fact that, in all Chinese people, the element of Drama is instilled to the very marrow — witness the minute children pretending to be asleep, or plying a fan, the seller of feather dusters posing in the sunlight, the young archers and sportsmen with the gestures of ballet dancers, and the sentry stopping the oncoming traffic with every fragment of his body. These snapshots, many of them taken in the grey fogs that hang about the wartime capital of Chungking, give only a picture of unoccupied China during its eighth year of war against aggression — but perhaps, in some of them, we can see the spirit of the essential, unchanging China.

C.B.

Threshing time, near Kunming

Village scene, Kwang-Chang

Washing scene in a village near Kunming

Villagers (and opposite) of Sze-Chwan Province show interest in foreign visitors

Bamboo

Wharfside, Chungking

Calligraphic décors

Policeman outside a magistrate's house, Chekiang Province

Recruits attending a lecture on self-government, Pihu, Fukien

Firemen at ready, Chungking

Tea house, Chengtu

*Luncheon at West China Union
University*

Basket-ball, Pihu

Yangtse sampans

Ming Sung Naval Dockyard, Chungking: boys sawing up pine trunks for planking

River scene, Kanshien

Carrying merchandise over the hills of Kiangsi Province

Villagers going to market, Kunming

Village street

Children paddling in Fu-Ho River, Kiangsi Province

Chungking orphans

Children of refugee government officials at co-educational school,
Shantung

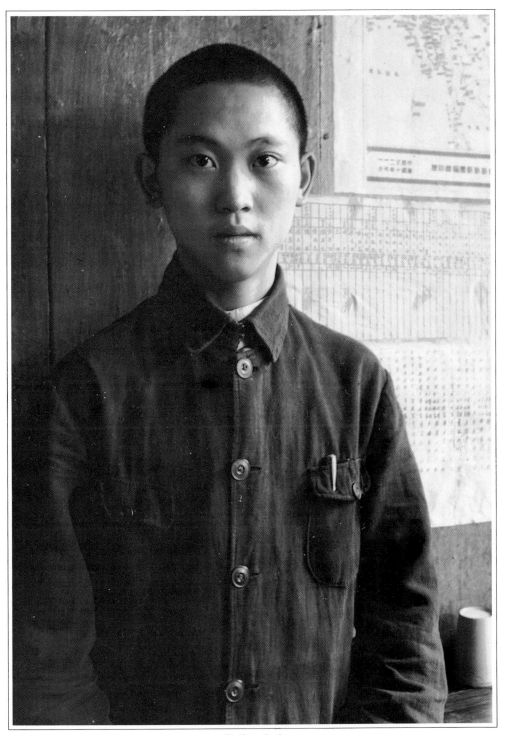

Police clerk

Cotton mill hands, Chungking

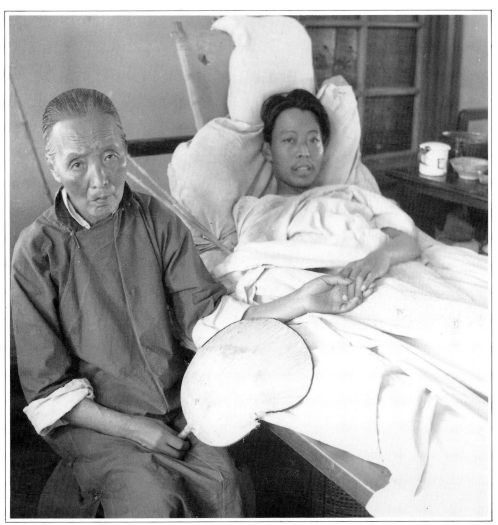

Mother and son

Noodle making, Sze-Chwan

The primitive method of making noodles by hand.
The lengths of noodles are stretched between poles for drying

Salt wells, Tseliuching

A salt mining town: Tseliuching

A deaf and dumb woman, with her wards, at the Poor People's Refuge, Changsha

Beggar picking over rags

REFUGE FOR DESTITUTES, CHANGSHA

Deaf mute at spinning wheel

117

Coolie boy

Kweilin

Kanshien

119

Toys and funeral offerings: paper money for coffins
and fly whisks

Decorations outside a Sze-Chwan shop celebrating its anniversary

Kunming

Chungking

Rickshaws in Chengtu

General Chang Chih-Chung

A fireman

A demonstration at Pihu Training Centre

Chinese surprise troops

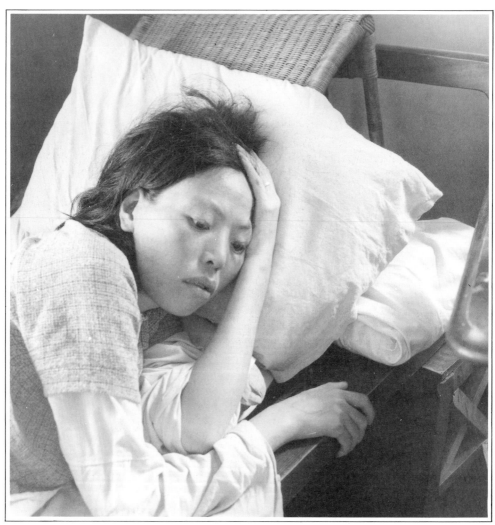

In the women's ward

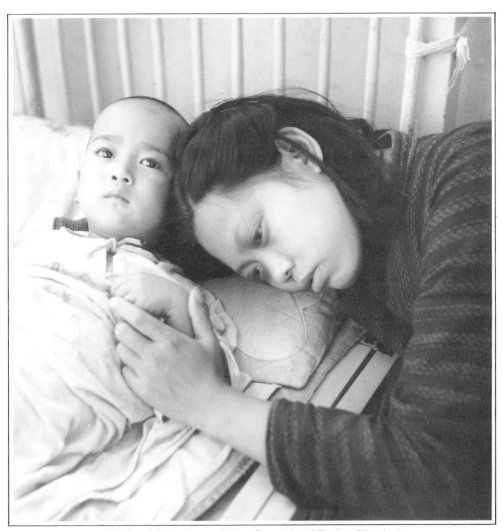

In the children's ward of a Canadian Mission Hospital

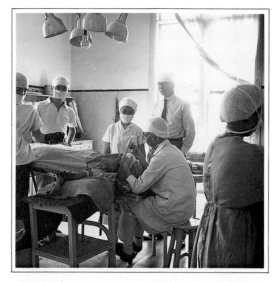

Amputation

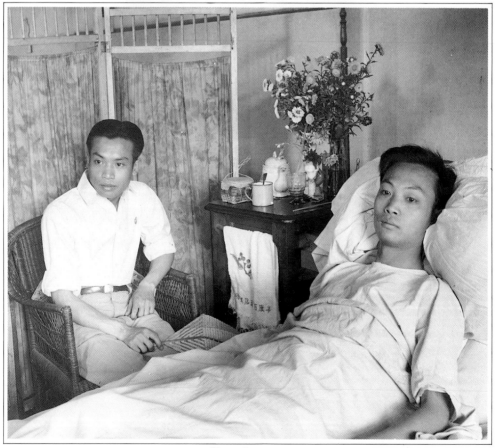

Convalescence

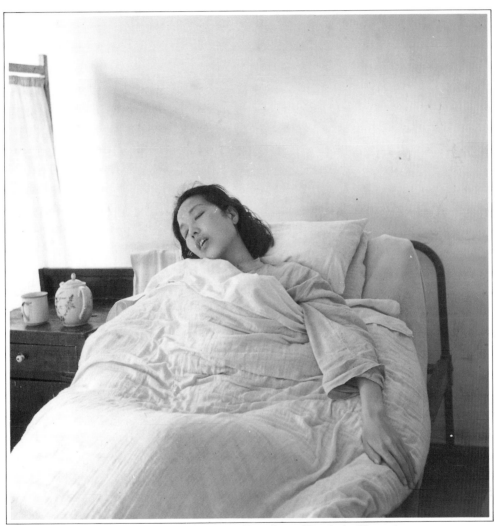

In the women's ward of the Red Cross Hospital, Changsha

Gateman

Gateman, Kincheng Bank Guest House

Near Chien Yang

Ricefields at Koloshan

Mill hands in the winding room of a cotton mill

Mr. Tai Chi-Tao, President of the Examination Council, in Government Building,
Chungking, during a session of the Chinese Government

*Tung tree in flower,
Lung-Chuan*

Kia-ling River, and a distant view of Chungking

Fukien landscape

A Chinese audience watching a performance at Pau Fou Tie theatre, Chengtu

Characters of the Chinese theatre

141

Mr Chow Chung-Yueh, Chinese scholar from Yunan Province

Professor Yang Hsien-Yi of Fuhtan University, with Mr. Lu-Chien, poet

Coolie

Ten-year-old with three-months-old sister

Shopkeeper, Pihu

144

*Peach seller,
Sze-Chwan Province*

Straw stacks in the courtyard of a farm near Kunming

145

Dr. Lu-Chien, Chinese poet

Professor T.K. Chuan, of Fuhtan University

Chinese commando

A march past at the Central Military Academy

General Wan-Yao-Luang takes the salute

The beggar

A flag maker, Chengtu

Mrs. K.C. Wu, wife of the Chinese Vice-Minister of Foreign Affairs

Mr. Fang Chan, Chief of Police, Chengtu

West China Union University, Chengtu: history students in the educational building

Sze-Chwan University: students leaving the mathematical building

Chinese girl guides

Temple in Sze-Chwan

Rice store

Sixty-five-year-old watchman

Temple assistant

Rickshaw coolie outside a telegraph office

Salt cleaning filter, Tseliuching

Stemming tobacco at Kan-Yung Brothers' factory at Chungking

Yangtse coolies

Sword-play demonstration

Tributary of the Mei-Kiang River, Kiangsi Province

Ningtu village pond, and Rosa Multiflora

Nursery School in disused temple near Peipei

The next generation

Boy with fan, Chengtu